HELP!

My Apartment Has a Kitchen

COOKBOOK

To Jody and Bart
for the countless hours they spent
eating our food

HELP!

My Apartment Has a Kitchen

COOKBOOK

100+ Great Recipes with Foolproof Instructions

KEVIN MILLS
AND NANCY MILLS

ILLUSTRATIONS BY
RICHARD A. GOLDBERG

HOUGHTON MIFFLIN COMPANY
Boston · New York

Visit our Web site: www.houghtonmifflinbooks.com.

Library of Congress Cataloging-in-Publication Data
Mills, Kevin
Help! my apartment has a kitchen cookbook: 100+ great recipes
with foolproof instructions / Kevin Mills and Nancy Mills;
illustrations by Richard A. Goldberg.
p.   cm.
Includes index.
ISBN 1-881527-63-8 (softcover)
1. Cookery. I. Mills, Nancy II. Title.
TX714.M555 1996
641.5—dc20   95-48198

Designed by Susan McClellan

Printed and bound in Canada by
Transcontinental Printing, Peterborough, Ontario
20 19 18 17 16 15

CONTENTS

My Discovery of the Kitchen

I HAD ALWAYS KNOWN OF THE EXISTENCE OF THE KITCHEN. It was the room with the fridge in it. As for cooking, it was someone else's problem. It was Mom's. But it's all a matter of perspective, I guess. From my vantage point, my mom seemed to disappear into the world of pots and pans and emerge an hour later with plates of steaming deliciousness. And all was well. I just had to show up at 6:30 and Mom

would strap on the feed bag. But as any good cynic will tell you, nothing good lasts forever. I went away to college and my mother didn't.

My first two years, I lived in a dorm, and believe me, nobody cooks in a dorm. We would have eaten articles of clothing before approaching a kitchen. We would even eat in a dining hall. But despite our many nutritional sacrifices, we were happy. My friends and I had proved cooking was for chumps, and Ramen soups were for the young and the cool.

Later my friends and I tired of dorm life, and we decided to spend our junior year in an apartment. Like other adults, we would pay rent, take out the garbage, vacuum and rejoice in our adulthood. We might even cook in the kitchen that our landlord had thoughtfully installed.

A LAS, BEFORE LONG, I was eating out almost every night. And on the nights I stayed in, I ordered out. And, once again, all was well. I was able to point at a menu and make a few grunting noises, and in return I was waited on and fed. It was just like home! Of course, I now had to pay, but I was too busy to worry about money. Meanwhile, the shiny microwave with all the buttons sat in the kitchen collecting dust. The oven was never opened. And all four burners remained unlit.

Day after day, my friends and I would enrich the local entrepreneurs who lived off our fear of the kitchen. And the food we ate! I'm shocked we didn't get scurvy. The closest we got to fresh vegetables was pizza sauce. But we were young in those days and proud to rebel against the laws of nutrition.

If health wasn't an issue, money was. My restaurant lifestyle quickly drained my savings. With a sense of panic, I remembered my dad's parting advice: "Call if you need anything but money." My mom's final words popped into my head: "Good-bye, son. I love you. Should I give you some recipes?" At the time I had laughed. But now I said: "Ha ha ha . . . Help!"

I called home. My mother was stunned at my sudden interest in preparing my

own food. I neglected to tell her that my primitive survival instinct alone had forced me to call. Over the phone, she told me how to roast a chicken. I must admit, it sounded pretty easy. I agreed to give it a try, and I lived to tell the tale. (See Roast Chicken, page 220.)

Over the next few months, my mother sent me more recipes, each selected for its simplicity. And I gradually learned how to prepare my own food. Despite my need to eat, I wouldn't have stuck with cooking if it had been difficult.

MY MOM HAD THE IDEA FOR THIS COOKBOOK. I think she figured that if she could teach a kitchen illiterate like me to cook, there was no one who couldn't learn. I was skeptical, basically because I think of cookbooks as often as I think of picking up my dirty clothes. But we came up with a format that satisfied us both. We agreed there might be others like me who were forced into the kitchen by circumstances beyond their control, and these people needed a cookbook on their level. Thus, we decided that she would teach the world to cook, while I would be right there making jokes and making sure that she didn't get too fancy. And anything unclear in the recipes I would try to explain.

In addition to providing a list of foods to keep on hand so you won't starve (page 260), we've also rated our recipes Very Easy, Easy, Not So Easy. And in the section Cooking Basics Mom Had to Teach Me (opposite page), we deal with common questions like how to cut an onion without crying and what to do with leftovers. More than half our recipes are suitable for vegetarians, and we tell you how to adapt many of the other ones. For the very ambitious, we offer Menus for Entertaining (page 262) to help you figure out what goes with what.

We hope you appreciate our attempts to demystify cooking. So, go forth and cook, but don't forget to wash your hands.

—*Kevin Mills*

Cooking Basics Mom Had to Teach Me

What's the First Step in Cooking?

Read the whole recipe through before you start. You don't want to be in for any nasty surprises midway through. This happened to me when I was making Chicken Tikka (page 212), a dish that requires marinating for at least 15 minutes. When I made Gazpacho (page 50), a cold tomato soup, I couldn't wait to eat it—but I had to because the recipe said to refrigerate the completed soup for at least 2 hours before serving. The next time I made it, I didn't wait until just before I planned to serve dinner.

What Are the Most Useful Packaged Foods?

Even my mom doesn't make everything from scratch. Here are the packaged foods she uses all the time and never feels guilty about:

▼ Bottled lemon juice
▼ Bottled salsa
▼ Canned chicken and beef broth
▼ Canned black, kidney and garbanzo beans
▼ Canned green chilies
▼ Canned tomatoes
▼ Corn flake crumbs
▼ Frozen spinach
▼ Frozen peas
▼ Italian-style bread crumbs
▼ Pillsbury Pie Crusts
▼ Pizza sauce

How Do I Peel and Cut an Onion?

Here are four options to avoid crying like a baby:-

▼ While you are peeling the onion, hold it under cold water.

▼ Drop an unpeeled onion in boiling water and cook for 1 minute. Then peel.

▼ Store your onions in the refrigerator vegetable bin and peel while they're still cold.

▼ Wear a diver's mask, snorkel optional.

To Peel: Cut ¼-inch slices from the root and tip ends of the onion and discard them. Then make a vertical slice through the papery brown layers and the first white layer of the onion. Remove those layers together and discard them.

To Cut: It's bad enough that you're crying and your fingers smell bad. It shouldn't also take forever. To speed up, cut the onion in half and place the cut sides down on the cutting board. Cut ¼- or ½-inch slices, whatever the recipe calls for. If the recipe says "chopped" or "pieces" or "squares," then cut across the slices to the size required. Don't worry about making pieces identical. They shrink anyway.

How Do I Peel and Cut Garlic?

Garlic grows in bulbs, which are made up of individually wrapped sections called cloves. Don't use a bulb when only a clove is required, as my friend once did. Choose bulbs that are heavy and plump, not shriveled. Store them, uncovered, in the cupboard.

To Peel: Here are two options:

▼ Put the garlic clove on a cutting board, lay a wide knife blade on top of it and press hard. The clove will crumple out of its skin.

▼ Drop the garlic clove in boiling water for 5 seconds. The skin will slip right off.

To Cut: Put the knife point on the cutting board and the peeled garlic directly underneath the blade. Without touching the garlic with your fingers and keeping the knife point on the board, bring the blade up and down on the garlic until it's chopped as fine as you want. The pieces do not have to be identical in size.

WHAT IF I ONLY HAVE ONE POT?

If you've just discovered that your apartment has a kitchen but no pots and pans, don't despair. You can feed yourself with just one pot. And with the money you save from not ordering pizzas, you'll soon be able to buy more pots.

Meanwhile, take your cue from the two characters in an English comedy. Trapped in a country cottage, they tried cooking a chicken by stuffing it into a tea kettle. Their mistake was leaving the chicken whole. If they'd cut it into pieces, they could have had dinner.

Think creatively with whatever pot(s) you do have. Just because the recipe says, 'Begin heating the chicken broth in a medium-size pot," there's no reason you can't substitute a large pot or wok instead. Of course, the reverse won't always work. Cooking spaghetti noodles in a pot just large enough to boil four eggs would be difficult—unless you broke the noodles into 2-inch pieces. If I could have only one pot, I'd choose a soup pot. My mom would pick a wok.

HOW DO I DOUBLE OR HALVE A RECIPE?

Most recipes can be doubled or halved without difficulty, with the exception of pies and cakes. Points to keep in mind:

▼ If you double a cooked meat dish like Spaghetti Bolognese (page 101), the initial step of browning the meat will take nearly twice as long. The rest of the cooking time will be just a little bit longer. Once all parts of the dish begin to cook, they will cook at the same speed. Twice as much spaghetti doesn't take twice as long to cook. Once the water returns to the boil, it will cook in the time specified. However, it's less apt to stick together if you boil it in more water.

▼ Spices and seasonings shouldn't be randomly doubled because the resulting flavor may be too intense, or in the case of cayenne pepper or red pepper flakes, too hot. Start with one and one-half times the amount and taste-test before adding more.

▼ If you want to halve a recipe that calls for 1 egg, use 1 medium egg. If you're doubling a recipe that calls for 1 egg, you could either use 2 eggs or 1 extra-large or jumbo egg.

Should I Blindly Trust My Oven?

Ovens can be ornery creatures. They don't always heat at the temperature they say they're heating at. If your chocolate chip cookies are burned after their normal 6-minute cooking time, your oven temperature is hotter than it should be. If the cookies are still raw, the oven isn't hot enough. Buy an oven thermometer (they cost $4 to $8) and hang it on one of the oven racks. It tells you what temperature the oven is really at. Adjust the dial accordingly.

What If I Have a Disaster?

A million bad things can happen. Option number 1 is to sulk and go to bed hungry. Option number 2 is to be creative.

If the food has fallen all over the floor and been licked by the dog, order a pizza. Or do like my mom did when she dropped a turkey as she was taking it out of the oven. Thinking fast, she picked it up off the floor and put it on the carving board. Luckily, no one saw her do it. She confessed only years later. Another time, she baked a chocolate cake in an angel food cake pan, which has a large hole in the middle. She claims the directions said to cool the cake by setting it upside down on the neck of a large glass soda bottle, which she did. And before too long, large clumps of cake fell to the counter. Instead of throwing it out—it was chocolate, after all—she invented a new dessert, a chocolate cake sundae. She put chunks of cake and ice cream in dishes and poured fudge sauce over the top, and everybody asked for seconds.

How Do I Get a Whole Meal on the Table at Once?

Read through each recipe you plan to cook and make a schedule for yourself. Work backwards from the time dinner will be served so you'll know when to start each dish.

Plan a menu that doesn't require every dish to be made at the last minute. There are some that you can prepare early and then reheat—including most soups, Sauerbraten (page 184) and Chicken Cacciatore (page 205). Many others are supposed to be served at room temperature or cold—including Thai Pasta Salad (page 70), Potato Salad (page 78), Guacamole (page 28) and most desserts. Some foods can be cooked and kept hot for up to 30 minutes before putting on the table—including Spicy Bean Dip (page 30), Roast Chicken (page 220) and Parsley Rice (page 142).

But wait! You're not going to get off that easily. Certain dishes will suffer unless they're served as soon as they're ready—including Nachos (page 34), Skillet French Fries (page 137), Pan-Fried Steak (page 180) and all the hot pasta recipes. If one of these is part of your menu, try to make sure it's the only one.

For more ideas, see Menus for Entertaining (page 262).

How Can I Convert a Dish for a Carnivore into One for a Vegetarian?

▼If the only animal ingredient in a recipe is either chicken or beef broth, substitute a vegetable bouillon cube and water.

▼Substitute tofu for the meat ingredient.

▼In recipes where meat is not essential, make the recipe without the meat, serve the vegetarian portion and then add the meat. Try this with such recipes as Slice-and-Dice Ham and Vegetable Soup (page 56) or Thai Pasta Salad (page 70).

How Should I Deal with Leftovers?

Some people hate leftovers, but I look on them as an opportunity not to have to cook another day. Sometimes, in fact, I double a recipe in order to have leftovers. There are three ways to deal with leftovers:

▼ **Eat Them Tomorrow**

Refrigerate leftovers in a covered container so they don't dry out. If you're not planning to eat them within three days, choose one of the following alternatives.

▼ **Transform Them**

Most leftovers can be used as part of another dish. For instance, roast chicken, ham, roast beef, rice and potatoes can be cut up and tossed into a salad, added to a can of chicken broth or stuffed inside a tortilla. When added to 2 cups of water or vegetable bouillon, leftover salads, pasta dishes or stir-fries suddenly become soups.

▼ **Freeze Them**

I used to just put leftovers in the fridge and forget about them. Every now and then I'd clean out the shelves and say, "Yuck!" and throw everything away. I must have one foot in the grave because I'm starting to plan ahead. I might even begin labeling those mystery containers.

Almost everything you cook from this book can be frozen, with the exception of dishes containing fresh vegetables and fruits, hard-cooked eggs and mayonnaise. Here are some tips:

▼ Use plastic containers, plastic bags, plastic wrap or heavy-duty foil to store food.

▼ Freeze in 1- or 2-portion servings. For instance, if you made Sauerbraten (page 184) and have a lot left, divide it into several batches with portions of gravy and freeze.

▼ Don't fill a container to the top, because the contents will expand when frozen and the lid will pop off. Leave ½ inch of extra space.

▼ Eat frozen leftovers within two months. They're not like diamonds. They don't last forever.

Thawing Tips

▼ The night before you want to eat a package of frozen leftovers, move it from the freezer to the refrigerator. By dinnertime, it should be fairly well thawed. Take Sauerbraten (page 184), for instance. Heat the meat and gravy in a small pot over medium-low heat for 5 to 10 minutes until hot. If it's still partly frozen, it will take slightly longer to heat.

▼ Soups or foods that have been frozen in gravy can be reheated while they are still frozen. Remove the food from its container by placing the covered container under hot running water for about 30 seconds, or until the contents easily slide out. Heat in a pot over low heat and stir until the contents begin to thaw. Add 1 to 2 tablespoons extra water, if necessary, but not much more, or you will dilute the flavor. Continue stirring until the food is hot.

▼ If wrapped in foil, individual servings of chicken, meat, potatoes or quiche can go directly from the freezer to the oven in the foil. Heat at 350 degrees for about 20 minutes. Unwrap carefully to see if the food is hot enough. If not, rewrap and continue heating for another 5 to 10 minutes.

▼ If you have a microwave oven, follow its instructions for thawing food.

Key Weights and Measures

3 teaspoons = 1 tablespoon	1 stick butter or margarine = ½ cup
4 tablespoons = ¼ cup	1 cup = 8 fluid ounces = ½ pint
8 tablespoons = ½ cup	16 ounces = 1 pound

RATING THE RECIPES

How EASY IS EASY? I've rated the recipes according to how easy they are to make. Very Easy recipes require little time and effort. Often, the most complicated part of making them is buying the ingredients. Preparation time usually takes less than 10 minutes.

Easy recipes take a little more effort. No part of the recipe is difficult to do, and there are just a few steps. Preparation time is usually between 10 to 20 minutes.

Not So Easy recipes require effort. The ones I've included are those I love so much that I don't mind. No store-bought substitute comes close to tasting as good. And often, the quantity is enough to last for several meals.

VERY EASY

EASY

▼ ▼ ▼

Not So Easy

APPETIZERS

WHY WOULD YOU EVER MAKE AN APPETIZER? By definition, it is food served before more food, and that means cooking twice. Under most circumstances, I just don't do that. So when I cook an "appetizer," that's what I'm having for dinner. Many's the evening that my girlfriend and I have set the table, lit some candles and settled down to a big bowl of bean dip. Or a whole loaf of garlic bread. Yummy.

However, there is one exception to my one-item-per-meal rule. If I'm cooking for company, I tend to make an appetizer. Some may think that I do this to impress my guests. But it's actually to protect myself in case I burn the main course. If you make two dishes, that increases the chances that one of them will be good. When you're an amateur cook, you don't want to pin all of your hopes on one pot of spaghetti. At worst your guests will still be able to say, "At least the dip was good."

Recipes

ANTIPASTO

SERVES: 4-6

Preparation Time: 20 minutes ▼ Cooking Time: None ▲ Rating: Very Easy

ANTIPASTO IS A MINI-BUFFET of seemingly unrelated cold vegetables, cheeses and meat, usually served with a salad dressing. It's a showpiece, not something you'd make for yourself and eat on your way out the door. You might make Antipasto as an appetizer for a dinner party or a gathering on Super Bowl Sunday.

You can't just throw the ingredients down in a lump. A little conceptual design helps. However, no cooking is required, which is always a bonus. Another reason this dish is good is that you can leave out any of the ingredients you don't like, which for me is olives.

½   head iceberg or leaf lettuce
¼   pound thinly sliced salami
¼   pound thinly sliced provolone or mozzarella cheese
12   cherry tomatoes
8   green olives
8   black olives
¼   pound marinated mushrooms, drained (see Mom Tip 1)
1   15-ounce can garbanzo beans (chick-peas), drained
1   6¼-ounce can tuna in oil or water, drained (see Mom Tip 1
      for Basic Tuna Salad, page 63)
1   6-ounce jar marinated artichoke hearts, drained
     Italian salad dressing (optional)
     French or Italian bread (optional)

Separate the lettuce leaves, rinse thoroughly and pat dry with paper towels. Cut or tear the leaves into 2-to-3-inch pieces and lay them neatly on a large plate.

Roll the slices of salami and cheese into cylindrical shapes and arrange them decoratively on the lettuce. Position the tomatoes, olives, mushrooms, garbanzo beans, tuna and artichoke hearts in sections on the lettuce. Pour some salad dressing over the garbanzo beans, if desired. Serve with French or Italian bread, if you like.

Mom Tip 1

▼

Marinated mushrooms
are available at the deli or in jars,
although I myself don't like the overly
sharp flavor of the jarred variety.

Mom Tip 2

▼

Al Dente Asparagus (page 148)
makes a nice addition to an
antipasto tray.

Cheese Easies

SERVES: 10-12 ▲ MAKES ABOUT 75 CHEESE EASIES

Preparation Time: 15 minutes ▼ Waiting Time: At least 1 hour

Cooking Time: 10-15 minutes ▲ Rating: Easy

WHAT'S A CHEESE EASY? It looks like a cookie but tastes like a cheese cracker. When I first made these, I absentmindedly poured in the whole package of onion soup mix. The result tasted more like ashtray remnants than anything to do with cheese. The next time, I measured every ingredient meticulously.

½   cup (1 stick) butter or margarine,
      softened to room temperature (see Mom Tip 1)

2   cups (8 ounces) shredded Cheddar cheese,
      at room temperature (see Mom Tip 2)

½   envelope dried onion soup mix

1   cup flour

Mix all the ingredients in a bowl until well combined. You will probably want to use your hands. This can be good exercise. The mixture will feel like Play-Doh but slightly greasy. Or combine the ingredients in a food processor and process continually until mixed.

Divide the dough into thirds and shape each into a 6-inch-long roll, 1 inch in diameter. They will look like big hot dogs. Refrigerate for at least 1 hour to make the dough easier to slice. Since each roll makes about 25 Cheese Easies, you'll probably want to freeze at least one roll for future use. Wrap any rolls you plan to freeze in foil, plastic or wax paper and freeze for up to 3 months.

Preheat the oven to 375 degrees.

Cut the remaining rolls into ¼-inch slices. Place on an ungreased baking sheet, leaving at least ½ inch of space between each slice. Bake for 10 to 15 minutes, or until they begin to brown. Check frequently during the last minutes so they don't burn. Use a spatula to transfer them to a serving dish and serve immediately. They taste good hot as well as at room temperature.

Mom Tip 1

▼

It's easier to mix up the
ingredients if the butter/margarine
and shredded cheese are at
room temperature.

Mom Tip 2

▼

You can shred
Cheddar cheese by hand
on a grater or in a blender or food
processor. Use the food processor's
shredding disk or cut the cheese
into 1-inch cubes and process
it into tiny pieces.

Garlic Bread

SERVES: 4

Preparation Time: 15 minutes ▼ **Cooking Time:** 15 minutes ▲ **Rating:** Easy

MY MOM ALWAYS SAID, "Don't fill up on bread." But now that I'm on my own, I can eat 15 slices of Garlic Bread before dinner. The only warning I have, other than about the potentially fatal breath, is to make this dish the day you buy the bread. Recently, I left a loaf of French bread in the fridge for three days, and when I took it out to slice, it was as solid as a baseball bat. I now keep it by the front door to beat off intruders.

1	loaf French or Italian bread
½	cup (1 stick) butter or margarine
2	garlic cloves or ½ teaspoon garlic powder
1	teaspoon dried oregano
1	teaspoon Schilling Salad Supreme Seasoning (see Mom Tip 1)

Preheat the oven to 375 degrees.

Cut the bread into 1-inch slices, not quite cutting through the bottom crust, so the slices stay attached to one another. Melt the butter or margarine in a small pot over medium heat. As soon as it is melted, remove the pot from the heat.

Peel and finely chop the garlic and add it to the pot. Add the oregano and salad seasoning and mix well.

Cut a piece of aluminum foil about 4 inches longer than the length of the bread. Place the bread in the center of the foil and, with a spoon, apply ½ teaspoon butter mixture to each side of each slice. It doesn't have to go on evenly. Spread any leftover butter mixture on top of the loaf. Wrap the foil around the loaf, twisting the ends (**see Mom Warning**). Bake for 15 minutes, or until steam escapes when you unwrap the foil. The bread will be crisp on the outside, soft in the middle. Serve immediately.

Mom Tip 1

▼

If you don't have a bottle of Schilling Salad Supreme Seasoning (available in the spice section at the grocery store), substitute ½ teaspoon grated Parmesan cheese, ¼ teaspoon celery seed, ⅛ teaspoon paprika and ⅛ teaspoon black pepper.

Mom Tip 2

▼

To make individual garlic breads, use rolls. Cut them in half lengthwise, and spread each half with up to 1 tablespoon of the butter mixture. Bake as directed for 10 minutes. Store any extra butter mixture in a covered dish in the refrigerator to use for future garlic breads.

Mom Warning

▼

Make sure the Garlic Bread is fully enclosed in foil or it will get hard and dry during baking.

GUACAMOLE

SERVES: 2

Preparation Time: 10 minutes ▼ Cooking Time: None ▲ Rating: Very Easy

I DON'T KNOW WHY THEY CALL an avocado a vegetable when it's actually a dip. The lemon juice and salsa help round out the taste, but they're not fundamental. Nature did all the work here.

Make sure when you buy an avocado that it is soft to the touch but not squishy. I inadvertently bought one that was rock hard. When I tried to mash it, I couldn't. I rolled up my sleeves and began squeezing the resistant green baseball, but all I ended up with were shards of solid avocado. My mom told me to grind it up in the blender or food processor, add extra lemon juice and salsa and not tell anyone.

    1   ripe avocado (see Mom Tip 1)
    1-2 tablespoons salsa
    1   tablespoon lemon juice
         Dash salt

Cut the avocado lengthwise the whole way around and twist to separate the halves. Toss the pit; peel both halves.

Put the avocado halves in a bowl and mash them with a fork. Add 1 tablespoon of the salsa, the lemon juice and salt. Mix and taste. If the guacamole isn't spicy enough, add another tablespoon salsa, mix and taste again.

Eat the guacamole within a few hours because it tends to turn brown (**see Mom Tip 2**). If you're not going to consume it immediately, cover the dish with plastic wrap and refrigerate.

Mom Tip 1

▼

The key to guacamole
is having an avocado that is
fully ripe but not so overripe that
the inside is full of gross brown spots.
When you press the skin of a ripe
avocado, the flesh underneath is soft.
If the avocado is too ripe, the skin will
look shriveled and/or have brown
discoloration. Avoid these.
If you have an unripe avocado,
you can speed up the ripening process
by placing the avocado in a small
paper bag, closing the top and
letting it sit on your counter for
2 days. Bags magically
ripen avocados.

Mom Tip 2

▼

Serve with tortilla chips
or sliced raw vegetables,
such as carrots (peeled),
cucumbers (peeled),
celery, red or green bell
peppers, radishes, mushrooms
and zucchini.

SPICY BEAN DIP

SERVES: 8

Preparation Time: 10 minutes ▼ Cooking Time: 30 minutes ▲ Rating: Very Easy

I EAT SPICY BEAN DIP all the time as a snack. It's pretty much foolproof. However, this dip is very hot when it comes out of the oven. In my haste to wolf it down, I have sometimes scorched the roof of my mouth.

1	15-ounce can refried beans (see Mom Tip 1 for Nachos, page 35)
1	8-ounce package cream cheese (see Mom Tips 1 and 2)
1	cup sour cream (see Mom Tip 2)
1	tablespoon chili powder
¼	teaspoon cayenne pepper or 10 drops hot pepper sauce (less if you don't like spicy food)
3	scallions
½	cup shredded Cheddar or Monterey Jack cheese
	Tortilla chips

Preheat the oven to 350 degrees.

Combine the refried beans, cream cheese, sour cream, chili powder and cayenne pepper or hot pepper sauce in a 1-quart ovenproof dish. Mix thoroughly.

Wash the scallions. Cut off the root tips and top 2 inches of the green ends and discard them. Cut the remaining white and green parts into ¼-inch pieces and stir them into the bean mixture. Sprinkle the cheese on top.

Cover the dish with an ovenproof lid or a piece of aluminum foil tucked around the top edge. Bake for 30 minutes, or until the mixture bubbles. Serve with tortilla chips.

Mom Tip 1

▼

To stir in the cream cheese
more easily, take it out of the
refrigerator several hours beforehand.
Or cut it into small pieces before
adding. You can also use
soft cream cheese.

Mom Tip 2

▼

Light cream cheese and
light sour cream are perfectly
acceptable in this dip.

Mexican Seven-Layer Dip

SERVES: 8-10

Preparation Time: 20 minutes ▼ Cooking Time: None ▲ Rating: Not So Easy

MAKING A SEVEN-LAYER DIP is like building a pyramid. There's no cooking. You just lay one ingredient on top of the next. Of course there's no need to stop at seven layers. You could empty out the fridge and build this dip right up to the ceiling. We can't vouch for the taste, though. It's also okay to skip some items and have a one-layer dip, but who wants to eat one layer of scallions?

1	large ripe avocado (see Mom Tip 1 for Guacamole, page 29)
2	tablespoons lemon juice
¼	teaspoon garlic powder
1	cup sour cream
2	teaspoons dry taco seasoning mix (see Mom Tip 1)
2	scallions
2	medium tomatoes
1	9-ounce can bean dip (see Mom Tip 2)
1	cup shredded Cheddar cheese
½	cup sliced black olives
	Tortilla chips

Cut the avocado lengthwise the whole way around and twist to separate the halves. Toss the pit; peel both halves. Cut into ¼-inch pieces, transfer to a small dish, sprinkle with the lemon juice and garlic powder and set aside.

Combine the sour cream and the taco seasoning mix in a small bowl and stir thoroughly. Set aside.

Wash the scallions. Cut off the root tips and top 2 inches of the green ends and discard them. Cut the remaining white and green parts into ¼-inch pieces and set aside.

Wash the tomatoes, cut them into ¼-inch squares and set aside.

Spread the bean dip thinly on a large dish, covering the entire surface. Arrange the avocado pieces on top, discarding any juice. Spread the seasoned sour cream on top of the avocado pieces. Sprinkle the shredded cheese on the sour cream. Add a layer of tomatoes, a layer of black olives and a layer of scallions. Serve with a large bowl of tortilla chips.

Mom Tip 1

▼

Taco seasoning mixes
are sold in foil packets in the
Mexican food aisle of the grocery
store. They include such spices
as chili powder, paprika, garlic,
cumin and onion.

Mom Tip 2

▼

Bean dip is usually located
in the potato chip-pretzel aisle.
If you can't find it, you can substitute
an 8-ounce can of vegetarian refried
beans mixed with ¼ teaspoon
hot pepper sauce.

NACHOS

SERVES: 2

Preparation Time: 10 minutes (*plain nachos*)   ▼   15-20 minutes (*heavy-duty nachos*)

Cooking Time: 5 minutes   ▲   Rating: Very Easy

NACHOS ARE A TRADITIONAL SNACK at sporting events and at late-night artery-clogging sessions. When I was growing up, I used to think that they were called "Machos." I guess you could add a handful of hot chilies and make "Macho Nachos," but that's not advised unless you really have something to prove.

15-20	tortilla chips
1	cup shredded Cheddar or Monterey Jack cheese

Optional Extras

1	8-ounce can vegetarian refried beans (see Mom Tip 1)
1	scallion
1	small ripe avocado or ½ large ripe avocado (see Mom Tip 1 for Guacamole, page 29)
1-2	tablespoons sliced black olives
	Salsa
	Sour cream

Preheat the oven to 425 degrees (see Mom Tip 2).

Place the tortilla chips in a single overlapping layer on a baking sheet or ovenproof platter.

For plain nachos, cover the tortilla chips with cheese and bake for about 5 minutes, or until the cheese melts (see Mom Warning).

For heavy-duty nachos, after placing the tortilla chips on the baking sheet/platter, cover them with spoonfuls of refried beans.

Wash the scallion. Cut off the root tip and the top 2 inches of the green end and discard them. Cut the remaining white and green parts into ¼-inch pieces. Sprinkle them onto the tortilla chips.

Cut the avocado lengthwise the whole way around. Twist to separate the halves. If you are using both halves, toss the pit. If you are using only one of the halves, wrap the half with the pit tightly in plastic and refrigerate. Use within 1 to 2 days. The pit helps keep the avocado from turning brown but is no guarantee. Peel the remaining half, cut it into ¼-inch squares and sprinkle the squares onto the tortilla chips.

Sprinkle the black olive slices onto the tortilla chips.

Cover the entire concoction with cheese and bake for about 5 minutes, or until the cheese melts (**see Mom Warning**).

You can pile spoonfuls of salsa and sour cream on top just before serving.

Mom Tip 1
▼

Regular refried beans are made with lard, so vegetarians should make sure they select vegetarian refried beans. The label should clearly state "vegetarian." By the way, refried beans are cooked, mashed and fried before they are canned.

Mom Tip 2
▼

For easy clean-up, cover the baking sheet or platter with aluminum foil before starting the recipe.

Mom Warning
▼

A watched cheese never burns. In other words, keep checking the nachos as they bake. Look in on them after 3 minutes and then each succeeding minute.

SHRIMP COCKTAIL

SERVES: I

Preparation Time: 10 minutes ▼ Cooking Time: None ▲ Rating: Very Easy

WILL SOMEBODY PLEASE TELL ME why shrimp cost so much? Are they rare? Do they outsmart the fishermen somehow? Or are stores just charging what the market will bear? Whatever the reason, when I'm rich, I'm going to eat Shrimp Cocktail every day. At least the cocktail sauce is cheap and easy to make.

6   large cooked peeled shrimp (see Mom Tips 1 and 2)
1   large lettuce leaf (optional)
    About ⅓ cup ketchup
    About 1 teaspoon bottled horseradish (see Mom Tip 3)
½   teaspoon Worcestershire sauce
½   teaspoon lemon juice
    Dash hot pepper sauce

Rinse the shrimp and pat them dry with a paper towel. Restaurants serve shrimp on a bed of shredded lettuce. I usually skip the lettuce. To me, shrimp cocktail means dipping shrimp into sauce. If you want to use lettuce as a decoration, rinse the leaf, cut it into shreds and put in the bottom of a small bowl. Arrange the shrimp on top.

Make the cocktail sauce by combining the ketchup, horseradish, Worcestershire sauce, lemon juice and hot pepper sauce in a small bowl. Taste. If it's too spicy, add 1 teaspoon more ketchup. If it's not spicy enough, add ¼ teaspoon more horseradish and more hot pepper sauce. You can also add more Worcestershire sauce and lemon juice. Chill for 1 hour, if desired, or eat immediately.

Mom Tip 1

▼

Shrimp of any size taste good,
and smaller shrimp are often
considerably cheaper per pound.
The easiest thing to do is to buy
ready-to-eat shrimp, which are
already cooked and peeled.
You can specify the number you want.
Then all you have to do is put
them on the plate and eat.
The second easiest way is to buy
prepackaged frozen shrimp, which
are usually already cooked
and peeled (check the label).
Cooked shrimp are pink.
Raw shrimp are bluish-white.
Take out the number of shrimp you
need and plunge them into boiling
water for 30 seconds, or until they
become soft. Don't cook them any
longer or they will get tough.
If you plan to serve them
immediately, cool them first by letting
them sit in a bowl of ice water for
5 minutes. Then drain and serve.
Shrimp also come in cans,
but I don't like their tinny taste.

Mom Tip 2

▼

Raw unpeeled shrimp are
cheaper. Cook, then peel them.
Place the shrimp in a pot of boiling
water. Wait for the water to return to
boiling and then begin to time them.
Small shrimp cook in 1 to 2 minutes.
Large shrimp take 3 to 5 minutes.
Giant shrimp take 5 to 6 minutes.
They should be pinkish and firm,
not mushy (which means they are
still raw). As soon as the shrimp
are cooked, drain them and run
them under cold water to
stop the cooking.

Mom Tip 3

▼

Bottled horseradish
can be found either in the
refrigerated section of the grocery
store near the cheese or on a
shelf near the ketchup.

Soups

MY MOM HAD A HARD TIME convincing me to try her soup recipes because soup was one food I thought I already knew how to cook. Early in my college experience, I had discovered Ramen noodles. They were the perfect meal for a young gastronomically disadvantaged student. For between 20 and 33 cents, I could get a brick of desiccated noodles and an ambiguously named "flavor pack." All I had to do was add water. It didn't taste very good, but it kept me from being hungry for a few hours.

So why would I want to take more than three minutes to make soup? It's the same reason I don't eat frozen pizza *every* night: Even the nutritionally immoral have their limits. And besides, I grew up eating homemade soups, and I liked them.

My mom promised that making real soup was almost as quick and easy as making Ramen noodles—and I would have three or four bowls' worth. The principle was the same: Start with meat or vegetables, and basically just add water (or even milk). And what are spices anyway but a fancy name for a "flavor pack"? I still keep some Ramen noodles around for emergencies, but I prefer making soup I can actually serve to other people.

Recipes

BACON AND TOMATO SOUP

SERVES: 2 AS A MEAL, 3 AS AN APPETIZER

Preparation Time: 10 minutes ▼ Cooking Time: 15 minutes ▲ Rating: Easy

In 1961, my mom was given this recipe in a nutrition class. Since that time, bacon has gotten a bad reputation from nutritionists, simply because it's almost all fat. Well, I'm not going to tell you to eat it if you don't want to, but it sure tastes good. I'll take a slice of bacon over a couple of rice cakes any day.

4	slices bacon (see Mom Tip 1)
1	small onion
1	tablespoon butter or margarine
2	tablespoons flour
1	15-ounce can ready-cut tomatoes (see Mom Tip 2)
	Dash black pepper
	Dash salt
1	bay leaf
2	cups milk

Cook the bacon in a medium-size pot over medium-high heat. When the bacon is crisp, about 10 minutes, remove it from the pot. Set aside to drain on a paper towel. Drain the bacon fat into an empty can and discard it.

Peel the onion and chop it into ½-inch pieces. Melt the butter or margarine in the same pot over medium heat. Don't worry about any bacon residue, as it will serve to flavor the soup. Add the onion and cook for about 5 minutes, stirring occasionally, until the onion begins to soften. Add the flour and stir until it is fully absorbed into the onion mixture. This stirring is important (see **Mom Warning**).

Add the tomatoes and their liquid, black pepper, salt and bay leaf and bring the mixture to a boil over high heat. Turn down the heat to medium and cook, uncovered, for 2 minutes. The mixture will begin to thicken. Add the milk and heat until the soup is hot but not boiling. Cut or break the cooked bacon into bite-size bits and drop into the soup. Remove and discard the bay leaf, and serve.

Mom Tip 1

▼

Bacon comes in ½- and 1-pound packages. Once opened, a package will keep for about 1 week. If you don't plan to use it up quickly, freeze it in 4-slice portions, well wrapped in foil. When buying bacon, look for a package that has more meat than fat. Check both sides of the package. Cardboard packages have a small flap on the back that can be lifted to examine the contents.

Mom Tip 2

▼

Ready-cut tomatoes are whole tomatoes cut up into pieces. They are not mashed up or in sauce form. They have one big advantage over whole tomatoes: Someone else cut them up for you. They aren't necessarily more expensive than whole tomatoes. If you can't get them, canned whole tomatoes are a fine substitute. Just cut them into pieces yourself.

Mom Warning

▼

Flour is a thickening agent, but it needs to be dissolved in oil, melted butter or margarine or cold water before it comes in contact with a hot liquid. Otherwise, instead of thickening, it will form unappetizing lumps.

CHEDDAR POTATO SOUP

SERVES: 2 AS A MEAL, 3 AS AN APPETIZER

Preparation Time: 10 minutes ▼ Cooking Time: 30 minutes ▲ Rating: Easy

MOST SOUPS ARE WATERY, with bits of vegetable or meat thrown in. This soup is more the consistency of a milk shake. Not that it tastes like one, though. It tastes more like a liquid baked potato, and it's filling enough to be a whole meal.

Because my girlfriend is a vegetarian and doesn't eat beef broth, I substitute a vegetable bouillon cube to keep her happy. I don't know exactly what's in these cubes, but they do provide flavor in some mysterious way.

1	medium onion
1	tablespoon butter or margarine
1	tablespoon flour
1	10½-ounce can condensed beef broth + 1 can water
	(or 1 vegetable bouillon cube + 2½ cups water; see Mom Tip 1)
1	large potato
1	cup shredded Cheddar cheese (see Mom Tip 2)
	Dash black pepper

Peel and thinly slice the onion. Melt the butter or margarine in a medium-size pot over medium heat. Add the onion and cook for about 5 minutes, stirring occasionally, until it begins to soften. Add the flour and stir constantly until it is fully absorbed (**see Mom Warning for Bacon and Tomato Soup, page 41**). Add the beef broth (or vegetable cube) and water and turn up the heat to high.

While the soup is coming to a boil, peel the potato and cut into ½-inch cubes. Add to the pot. It will take the soup a few minutes to return to a boil. When it does, turn down the heat to low, cover, and cook for 20 minutes, or until the potatoes are soft enough to be mashed.

Turn the heat off and, using the back of a large spoon, mash some of the potatoes into the broth. The rest can remain in cubes to vary the soup's texture.

With the heat still off, add the Cheddar cheese and stir for 1 to 2 minutes, or until the cheese has melted. Season with black pepper and serve.

Mom Tip 1

▼

Vegetable bouillon cubes,
individually wrapped in foil and
packed in boxes or plastic containers,
are located near the canned soups
at the grocery store.

Mom Tip 2

▼

Instead of Cheddar,
you can substitute
Monterey Jack or
Swiss cheese.

Chinese Hot and Sour Soup

SERVES: 4 AS A MEAL, 6 AS AN APPETIZER

Preparation Time: 20 minutes ▼ Cooking Time: 10-15 minutes ▲ Rating: Easy

How hot is "hot"? In this case, not very. And who would eat something called Sour Soup? Me. "Hot and sour" is an attempt to describe the peculiar taste of this Asian soup. The only two words that come to mind are "tangy" and "exotic," both of which I think should be eliminated from the English language. So let me put it this way: The vinegar and soy sauce fight it out for the title, but neither dominates.

The first time I ate tofu was in this soup. Previously, it had seemed like a poor substitute for meat. But since it takes on the flavor of whatever it's cooked with and I like the flavor of this soup, tofu disappeared from my will-not-eat list. Maybe sometime the same thing will happen to me with sushi.

8	fresh medium mushrooms or 8 dried shiitake mushrooms (see Mom Tip 1 for Spicy Chinese Pork, page 198)
4	scallions
2	10½-ounce cans condensed chicken broth + 2 cans water (or 2 vegetable bouillon cubes + 5 cups water; see Mom Tip 1 for Cheddar Potato Soup, page 43)
1	8-ounce can bamboo shoots, drained
1	14-ounce package tofu, drained (see Mom Tip 1)
¼	cup white vinegar
2	tablespoons soy sauce
2	tablespoons cornstarch or ¼ cup flour
¼	cup cold water
2	eggs (any size)

If you're using fresh mushrooms, wash them and cut away and discard the bottom ¼ inch of the stems. Slice the mushrooms thin and set aside. If you're using dried shiitake mushrooms, put them in a cup or small bowl and cover with water. Let them soak for 20 minutes, or until they are soft enough to cut. Then slice them as thin as possible and set aside. Discard the tough stems and soaking liquid.

Wash the scallions. Cut off the root tips and top 2 inches of the green ends and discard them. Cut the remaining white and green parts into ¼-inch pieces and set aside.

Begin heating the chicken broth (or vegetable cubes) and water in a large pot over high heat. When it comes to a boil, add the mushrooms and bamboo shoots. Turn down the heat to medium and cook, uncovered, for 5 minutes.

While the soup is cooking, cut the tofu into ½-inch cubes. Add the tofu, vinegar and soy sauce to the soup; stir and cook for another 5 minutes.

Mix the cornstarch or flour with the cold water in a small bowl until it becomes a thick paste (**see Mom Warning**). Add it to the soup and stir until the mixture boils and thickens slightly.

Beat the eggs in a bowl. Pour the beaten eggs slowly through the tines of a fork into the soup. The tines help separate the eggs so that they cook in thin strands rather than in large clumps. Add the scallions and serve.

Mom Tip 1

▼

Tofu comes in three consistencies: soft, regular, firm. I always use firm, but for this soup, the consistency doesn't really matter.
The most common package size is 14 ounces. If you use only part of a package of tofu, store the rest in the refrigerator, covered with water, for 1 week.
Change the water every other day.

Mom Tip 2

▼

To use up leftover chicken or pork, cut up to 2 cups' worth into slivers and add to the soup when you add the tofu.

Mom Warning

▼

Never add cornstarch or flour directly to a hot liquid. It will make clumps of gooey paste instead of causing the soup to thicken.

Egg and Onion Soup

SERVES: 2 AS A MEAL, 4 AS AN APPETIZER

Preparation Time: 10 minutes ▼ Cooking Time: 25 minutes ▲ Rating: Very Easy

I WAS WARY OF CRACKING EGGS into a perfectly good soup and thus didn't want to cook this recipe. But one night there was nothing in the house to eat, so I took the requisite leap of faith and discovered the soup I now make once a week. When I can't think of anything else for dinner, I eat this as a one-dish meal. It's one of the easiest recipes in the book, and the ingredients are basic enough to keep regularly in the kitchen.

2   large onions

2   garlic cloves

3   tablespoons corn oil or olive oil

1   15-ounce can ready-cut tomatoes (see Mom Tip 2
    for Bacon and Tomato Soup, page 41)

1   tablespoon dried basil

1   tablespoon dried parsley

1   10½-ounce can condensed chicken broth + 1 can water
    (or 1 vegetable bouillon cube + 2½ cups water;
    see Mom Tip 1 for Cheddar Potato Soup, page 43)

4   large eggs

Peel and thinly slice the onions. Peel and finely chop the garlic. Heat the oil in a medium-size pot over medium heat. Add the onions and garlic and cook for about 5 minutes, stirring occasionally, until the onions begin to soften.

Add the tomatoes and their liquid, basil, parsley, chicken broth (or vegetable cube) and water. Bring to a boil and cook, covered, over medium-low heat for 15 minutes.

Remove the lid from the pot and crack the eggs, one at a time, into the boiling soup. Stir gently. The eggs should be at least partly submerged in the soup. Try not to break the yolks. Replace the lid and cook over low heat for another 5 minutes (**see Mom Warning**). You are "poaching" the eggs. The yolks will remain whole, and the whites will cook into a firm mass around them. But don't despair if the eggs break apart.

When serving, spoon 1 egg into each bowl and then ladle the soup into the bowls and serve.

Mom Tip

▼

For extra flavor,
sprinkle 1 teaspoon grated
Parmesan cheese into each bowl
of soup before serving.

Mom Warning

▼

If runny yolks bother you,
cook the eggs an extra 1 to 2 minutes
in the soup to be sure they're fully
cooked before serving.

FRENCH ONION SOUP

SERVES: 2

Preparation Time: 10 minutes ▼ **Cooking Time:** 35 minutes ▲ **Rating:** Easy

EVERY TIME I CUT ONIONS, I cry like I just saw *Bambi* for the first time. Nothing helps: cutting them under running water, cutting while wearing swimming goggles or even cutting while listening to Led Zeppelin. I suppose I could just keep my eyes shut, but then I might cry for another reason (see How Do I Peel and Cut an Onion? page 10).

Once I refined my onion-cutting skills, I realized I had other problems. The first time I cooked this soup, it boiled down to the consistency of pancake syrup. I woke up in the middle of the night screaming, "I forgot to add the can of water!" Eventually I read the directions and got it right. Overconfidence has been my undoing on several occasions.

2	medium onions
1	garlic clove
1	tablespoon butter or margarine
1	tablespoon olive oil
1	tablespoon flour
1	10½-ounce can condensed beef broth + 1 can water (or 1 vegetable bouillon cube + 2½ cups water; see Mom Tip 1 for Cheddar Potato Soup, page 43)
1	bay leaf
¼	teaspoon dried thyme
2	slices toasted French bread (see Mom Tip 1)
¼	cup shredded (or 2 slices) Swiss, Cheddar or mozzarella cheese

48
▼

Peel and thinly slice the onions. Reach for a handkerchief. Peel and finely chop the garlic. Heat the butter or margarine and oil in a medium-size pot over medium heat. Add the onions, turn the heat to low and cook for about 10 minutes, stirring occasionally. Add the garlic and cook for another 5 minutes (**see Mom Warning**). The mixture will be very soft and golden-colored.

Preheat the oven to 375 degrees.

Add the flour and stir carefully until it is fully absorbed into the onion mixture. Add the beef broth (or vegetable cube) and water, bay leaf and thyme. Cook, covered, over medium-low heat for 15 minutes. Remove and discard the bay leaf.

Place 2 ovenproof bowls (**see Mom Tip 2**) on a baking sheet. The baking sheet serves as a tray, making it easier to remove the hot soup bowls from the oven. Ladle the soup into the bowls, add a slice of French bread to each bowl and cover the bread with the cheese. Put the baking sheet into the oven and bake for 5 minutes, or until the cheese melts.

If your bowls are not ovenproof, do not put them in the oven. Forget about the French bread and add the cheese to the bowls before adding the soup. Serve hot.

Mom Tip 1

▼

Instead of French bread,
you can substitute
leftover Garlic Bread
(page 26).

Mom Tip 2

▼

Ovenproof means
"safe to use in the oven."
Regular china can't stand the
high heat of an oven and will crack,
but ovenproof china, which has been
specially treated and is labeled
"oven-to-table," can be used.
Metal kitchen bowls can be
used in the oven; plastic
bowls can't.

Mom Warning

▼

When frying the garlic,
don't let it get brown and crispy
because it will develop
a bitter flavor.

GAZPACHO

SERVES: 3 AS AN APPETIZER

Preparation Time: 15 minutes (*using a blender or food processor*) or 30 minutes (*by hand*)

Cooking Time: 30 seconds ▼ Waiting Time: 2 hours ▲ Rating: Easy

"GAZPACHO" sounds like a word Robin Williams might have used on the show *Mork and Mindy*. You know—"Shazbat," "Nanu Nanu," "Gazpacho." Well, it makes sense to me. Actually, gazpacho is a cold tomato soup—easy to make if you have a blender or food processor. It's perfect for hot summer days, when tomatoes are cheap, or even frigid winter nights, if you have a fever.

The first time I made Gazpacho, I didn't feel like waiting two hours to eat it. But after the first warm mouthful, I found it's like the difference between warm beer and cold beer. So I stuck a bowlful in the freezer for 20 minutes, and it tasted like I remembered. But for those more patient and less eager for ice crystals in their soup, it's best to refrigerate it for 2 hours.

3-4	large tomatoes
½	large cucumber
1	small onion
3	tablespoons olive oil
3	tablespoons red wine vinegar
½	teaspoon salt
⅛	teaspoon garlic powder
3-6	drops hot pepper sauce
	Dash black pepper
2	cups tomato juice—needed only if a blender or food processor is unavailable to make this soup

Start by removing the tomato skins, which are undesirable because they stick in your teeth. Here is an easy way to remove them (the tomato skins, not your teeth): Bring a large pot of water to a boil over high heat. Drop in the tomatoes and let them cook for 30 seconds, or until the skins begin to pucker. Remove them from the water and cut out the stem area of each tomato. Pull off and discard the skins. Cut the tomatoes into quarters and set aside.

Peel the cucumber and cut it lengthwise, exposing the seeds. With a spoon, scrape out and discard the seeds. Cut the cucumber into 2-inch chunks and set aside. Peel the onion, chop it into quarters and set aside.

To make in a blender or food processor, combine the tomatoes, cucumber, onion, oil, vinegar, salt, garlic powder, hot pepper sauce and black pepper in the appliance bowl (**see Mom Warning**).

Blend at high speed for about 20 seconds, or until the mixture is just slightly crunchy. If it's reluctant to blend, add ¼ cup water and blend again.

If you don't have a blender or food processor, cut the tomatoes, cucumber and onion into the smallest possible pieces and put them in a large bowl. Add the oil, vinegar, salt, garlic powder, hot pepper sauce, black pepper and tomato juice. Mix thoroughly.

Pour the mixture into a large bowl, cover, and refrigerate for at least 2 hours or overnight before serving (**see Mom Tip**).

Mom Tip

▼

Gazpacho thickens as it gets cold. If you prefer a thinner soup, add ½ cup cold water or cold tomato juice before serving.

Mom Warning

▼

Some food processors leak when filled beyond a certain point. If yours does, make the soup in batches. I prefer to make Gazpacho in a blender.

Hearty Lentil Soup

SERVES: 2 AS A MEAL, 4 AS AN APPETIZER

Preparation Time: 10 minutes ▼ Cooking Time: 30-40 minutes ▲ Rating: Easy

Y OU MAY WELL ASK, "What are lentils?" That was my first question too. The Lentil Advisory Board (a.k.a. my dad) calls them "little brown balls of protein punch." They are actually plant seeds, and they look like flakes of dried beans. But they taste better than beans, and they cook faster.

This lentil soup was one of my first recipes, discovered as a way of keeping my vegetarian girlfriend happy. I even cooked this dish in an attempt to impress her parents. They asked for the recipe.

1 medium onion

2 garlic cloves

2 medium celery stalks

1 tablespoon olive oil

1 15-ounce can ready-cut tomatoes (see Mom Tip 2
  for Bacon and Tomato Soup, page 41)

½ teaspoon dried oregano

 Dash black pepper

1 cup dried lentils (see Mom Tip 1)

2 10½-ounce cans condensed chicken broth + 1½ cans water

  (or 1 vegetable bouillon cube + 4 cups water; see Mom Tip 1

  for Cheddar Potato Soup, page 43)

 Grated Parmesan cheese

Peel the onion and cut it into ½-inch pieces. Peel and finely chop the garlic. Wash the celery stalks, trim and discard the ends and cut the stalks into ¼-inch slices.

Heat the oil in a large pot over medium heat. Add the onion, garlic and celery and cook for about 5 minutes, stirring occasionally, until the vegetables begin to soften. Add the tomatoes and their liquid, oregano, black pepper, lentils, chicken broth (or vegetable cube) and water.

Bring the mixture to a boil over high heat. Then turn down the heat to low and cook, covered, for 20 minutes. Test lentils to see if they're soft by tasting one. Undercooked lentils are like pebbles. If the lentils are too hard, cook for another 5 to 10 minutes.

When the soup is ready, it will be very thick. However, if it's too thick, add ½ to 1 cup more water. Ladle into bowls, sprinkle with Parmesan cheese and serve.

Mom Tip 1

▼

Dried lentils, which are
usually brownish-green but
sometimes orange, are packaged in
1-pound bags and are stocked next
to the rice and dried beans.
In Indian, Middle Eastern
and French cuisines, lentils are
an alternative to rice
or potatoes.

Mom Tip 2

▼

To turn Hearty Lentil Soup
into a main dish for
nonvegetarians, add
some slices of cooked
sausage.

Mexican Corn Chowder

SERVES: 2 AS A MEAL, 3 AS AN APPETIZER

Preparation Time: 5 minutes ▼ Cooking Time: 15-20 minutes ▲ Rating: Easy

WHEN I THINK OF CHOWDER, I think of *Moby Dick*. But chowder doesn't have to conjure up images of peg legs and white whales. It doesn't even have to have fish in it. It just has to be thick. You can stand your spoon up in a bowl of Mexican Corn Chowder, and it has plenty of flavor, thanks to the chilies.

1	medium onion
2	medium celery stalks
2	tablespoons corn oil
½	teaspoon ground cumin
1	tablespoon flour
1	15-ounce can creamed corn
½	4-ounce can diced green chilies, drained (see Mom Warning)
2	cups milk
½	teaspoon salt
¼	teaspoon black pepper
1	cup shredded Monterey Jack cheese
	Handful tortilla chips, whole or broken (optional)

Peel and finely chop the onion. Wash the celery stalks, trim and discard the ends and cut the stalks into ¼-inch slices.

Heat the oil in a medium-size pot over medium heat. Add the onion and celery and cook for about 5 minutes, stirring occasionally, until the vegetables begin to soften.

Add the cumin and flour and stir carefully until both are fully absorbed into the onion/celery mixture. Add the corn, chilies, milk, salt and black pepper and stir thoroughly.

Cook, uncovered, over medium-low heat, stirring occasionally, for 8 to 10 minutes, or until the soup thickens. Stir in the cheese and cook for another 1 to 2 minutes, or until the cheese melts and the soup is hot but not boiling (**see Mom Tip**). Ladle into bowls, sprinkle on a few tortilla chips, if you like, to provide crunch, and serve.

Mom Tip

▼

If the soup is too thick,
add an extra ½ cup milk or water.
When reheating, bring the soup
just to a boil and serve.

Mom Warning

▼

If you dislike spicy food,
add fewer green chilies.
Experiment with ½ teaspoon
to start. Taste the soup before adding
more. These chilies aren't terribly
hot, but they do add zing. Don't
confuse them with canned
or bottled jalapeños,
which *are* hot.

Slice-and-Dice Ham and Vegetable Soup

SERVES: 2 AS A MEAL, 4 AS AN APPETIZER

Preparation Time: 15 minutes ▼ Cooking Time: 20 minutes ▲ Rating: Not So Easy

A LOT OF SOUPS leave me waiting for the next course. This soup, however, practically begs to be eaten with a fork. It started out as a way to use leftover ham. Now I buy ham just so I can make this soup, although it turns out to be just as good and almost as filling without the ham.

1	medium celery stalk
1	medium carrot
1	small onion
1	garlic clove
2	tablespoons corn oil or olive oil
1	teaspoon dried basil
½	teaspoon dried thyme
⅛	teaspoon black pepper
	Dash salt
1	cup bite-size pieces ham (see Mom Tip 1)
1	15-ounce can ready-cut tomatoes (see Mom Tip 2 for Bacon and Tomato Soup, page 41)
2	cups water
¼	cup small pasta shapes, uncooked couscous or bulgur (see Mom Tip 2)
	Grated Parmesan cheese

Wash the celery and peel the carrot. Trim and discard the ends and cut the rest into ¼-inch slices. Peel and finely chop the onion and garlic.

Heat the oil in a medium-size pot over medium heat. Add the celery, carrot, onion and garlic and cook for about 5 minutes, stirring occasionally, until the vegetables begin to soften.

Add the basil, thyme, black pepper, salt, ham, tomatoes and their liquid, water and pasta, couscous or bulgur and stir. Bring the soup to a boil over high heat. Turn down the heat to medium-low and cook, covered, for 15 minutes, or until the pasta or grains are soft. If the soup is too thick, add ½ cup more water. Ladle into bowls, sprinkle with Parmesan cheese and serve.

Mom Tip 1

▼

If you don't have any
leftover ham, buy a ham steak.
Any extra ham can be frozen.

Mom Tip 2

▼

Couscous and bulgur
(cracked wheat) are often found
with the dried beans and rice or in
the specialty food section. You could
substitute ½ cup leftover
cooked rice instead.

Mediterranean Vegetable Soup

SERVES: 2 AS A MEAL, 4 AS AN APPETIZER

Preparation Time: 15 minutes ▼ Cooking Time: 25 minutes ▲ Rating: Not So Easy

THE ONLY TIME I went to the Mediterranean, my parents told me that all I wanted to eat was sand. Of course, I was two years old. They were off eating Mediterranean Vegetable Soup. Since then, my tastes have become more like my parents'. But whenever I drive past a sandbox, my mouth still waters.

I have yet to return to the Mediterranean. Meanwhile, I think about future travels when eating this soup, which has Mediterranean touches: fresh vegetables, olive oil and lots of garlic.

1	large onion
2	tablespoons olive oil
1	large potato
1	medium zucchini
2	cups water
1	15-ounce can ready-cut tomatoes (see Mom Tip 2 for Bacon and Tomato Soup, page 41)
10	strands uncooked spaghetti
¼	cup fresh or frozen (not thawed) peas
3	garlic cloves
1	teaspoon dried basil
⅛	teaspoon black pepper
	Dash salt
1	large egg
	Grated Parmesan cheese

Peel and thinly slice the onion. Heat the oil in a medium-size pot over medium heat. Add the onion and cook for about 5 minutes, stirring occasionally, until it begins to soften. While it is cooking, peel the potato and cut it into ½-inch cubes.

Add the potato to the pot and continue cooking for another 5 minutes, stirring occasionally. The potato will begin to soften, and the onion will be very soft. While the potato is cooking, wash the zucchini, trim and discard the ends and thinly slice.

When the onion/potato mixture has cooked for 10 minutes, add the zucchini, water and all but 4 chunks of the tomatoes, leaving these pieces and the juice in the can for use later in the recipe.

Break the spaghetti into 2-inch pieces, add to the pot and stir. Return the soup to a boil over high heat. Turn down the heat to medium-low and cook, covered, for 5 minutes. Add the peas and cook for another 5 minutes.

While the peas are heating, peel and finely chop the garlic and add to the tomato chunks and juice in the can. Add the basil, black pepper, salt and egg to the can, beat thoroughly and set aside.

When the soup has finished cooking, add 3 tablespoons of hot soup to the can containing the tomato mixture and stir.

Add the can contents to the soup (**see Mom Tip**). Heat for 1 minute, stirring constantly, just until the soup thickens. Remove from the heat, ladle into bowls, sprinkle with Parmesan cheese and serve.

Mom Tip

▼

Eggs are versatile. If they're treated with care,
they will even thicken soups. But you can't just add a beaten
egg directly to hot soup unless you want it to cook into
strands as in Chinese Hot and Sour Soup (page 44).
If you gradually heat the beaten egg by beating in a
small amount of hot liquid and then add it to the hot
soup, the egg will thicken the soup as it cooks.

SALADS

SALADS HAVE ALWAYS HAD AN IMAGE PROBLEM. I used to think that people would eat a salad only when they were denying themselves real food. A few lettuce leaves, a scrap of tomato and an olive thrown in for flavor. It's hard to imagine John Wayne moseying into a salad bar on the Rio Bravo and picking daintily among the alfalfa sprouts. His horse, maybe.

So when I came home from college once and my mom told me we would be having salad for dinner, I immediately plotted to make myself a frozen pizza when everyone else had left the dining room. But the dinner turned out to be Thai Pasta

Salad, which I ate with a smile on my face. In fact, I ate several helpings, and I didn't have any room for the pizza. The same betcha-can't-eat-just-one-plateful holds true for the rest of our salads. They definitely deserve space on the chuck wagon.

Recipes

Basic Tuna Salad

SERVES: 1 AS A SALAD, 2 AS A SANDWICH FILLING

Preparation Time: 5 minutes ▼ **Cooking Time:** None ▲ **Rating:** Very Easy

TUNA SALAD MAY NOT SOUND LIKE MUCH OF A MEAL, but when I started cooking for myself it was a relief to know I had at least one easy, quick, familiar dish that was impossible to ruin.

1	6¼-ounce can tuna (see Mom Tip 1)
1	teaspoon sweet relish
1-2	teaspoons mayonnaise
1	scallion

Drain and discard the liquid from the tuna. Transfer the tuna to a small bowl and separate it into flakes with a fork. Mix in relish and the mayonnaise to your taste.

Wash the scallion. Cut off the root tip and top 2 inches of the green end and discard them. Cut the remaining white and green parts into ¼-inch pieces and add to the tuna salad. Mix thoroughly and serve as a salad or as a filling for Grilled Cheese-Tuna-Pickle Sandwich (page 86). The salad can also be served chilled.

Mom Tip 1

▼

Buying a can of tuna—
who can fail at this task? But wait.
There are choices to make:
white or light, water-pack or
oil-pack, low-salt or regular.
Experiment with them all to see
which you like best. Light tuna has
a stronger flavor than white tuna.
Light is also cheaper.
Some prefer oil-pack tuna
because it's more moist and doesn't
need mayonnaise. One point to
remember: Anyone counting
calories should choose
tuna in water.

Mom Tip 2

▼

Other items to
add to your tuna salad
so it's not so basic:
1 stalk chopped celery,
½ chopped apple,
½ chopped cucumber,
1 chopped hard-cooked egg.

CREATIVE COLD BEEF SALAD

SERVES: 2 AS A MAIN COURSE

Preparation Time: 15 minutes ▼ Cooking Time: None ▲ Rating: Easy

RECENTLY I WAS LEFT WITH TWO POUNDS OF EXTRA MEAT after I ambitiously cooked a big roast beef. Even though roast beef is one of my favorite foods, how many days in a row can you eat roast beef sandwiches? On the fourth day, I ran out of bread, so I made a salad out of what was in the vegetable bin and added the rest of the beef. I was surprised it tasted good, but my mom later informed me that I'd reinvented cold beef salad.

½   pound cooked roast beef, chilled
¼   head red or green cabbage
4   large mushrooms
2   medium celery stalks
1   scallion
    Dash salt
    Dash black pepper
    Italian salad dressing

Cut the roast beef into bite-size pieces and put in a salad bowl.

Wash the outside of the cabbage and remove any old or discolored leaves. Slice the cabbage as thin as possible and then cut the slices into bite-size pieces. Add them to the bowl.

Wash the mushrooms and cut away and discard the bottom ¼ inch of the stems. Slice the mushrooms thin and add them to the bowl.

Wash the celery, trim and discard the ends, cut the rest into very thin pieces and add them to the bowl.

Wash the scallion. Cut off the root tip and top 2 inches of the green end and discard them. Cut the remaining white and green parts into ¼-inch pieces and add them to the bowl.

Sprinkle on some salt, black pepper and salad dressing, toss and serve. Or let it chill for a few hours or overnight to let the flavors blend.

Mom Tip

▼

You can add many different raw vegetables
to this salad: radishes, cucumbers, cherry tomatoes,
carrots, red bell peppers, spinach, zucchini,
bean sprouts, drained water chestnuts.
You could also add leftover cooked asparagus,
potatoes, green beans or broccoli.
The trick is not to let any one ingredient
overpower the salad.

Crunchy Black Bean Salad

SERVES: 2 AS A MAIN COURSE, 3-4 AS A SIDE SALAD

Preparation Time: 20 minutes ▼ Cooking Time: None ▲ Rating: Easy

I USED TO THINK that any meal without meat wasn't really a meal. It was a snack. Then I moved in with a vegetarian. At that point, I was forced to either cook two dishes or find a dish that would feed us both. I cabled my mom for more substantial vegetarian recipes, and she sent me this one. She had invented it one night when she couldn't find anything lying around for dinner. While it's not up there with pizza, Crunchy Black Bean Salad can be a tasty one-dish meal. It also works as a side salad.

1	15-ounce can black beans
4	radishes
2	scallions
½	large cucumber
½	ripe avocado (see Mom Tip 1 for Guacamole, page 29)
1	zucchini
½	cup walnut pieces
2-3	tablespoons Italian salad dressing

Drain the black beans in a strainer or colander. Rinse with water and drain again. Put the beans in a large bowl.

Wash the radishes, trim and discard the two ends and cut the rest into ¼-inch pieces. Add them to the bowl.

Wash the scallions. Cut off the root tips and top 2 inches of the green ends and discard them. Cut the remaining white and green parts into ¼-inch pieces. Add them to the bowl.

Peel the cucumber and cut it into ¼-inch pieces. Add them to the bowl.

Cut the avocado lengthwise the whole way around and twist to separate the halves. Wrap the half with the pit tightly in plastic and refrigerate it. Use within 1 to 2 days or it will turn brown. Peel the remaining half and cut it into ¼-inch pieces. Add them to the bowl.

Wash the zucchini, cut off and discard the ends and chop the remainder into ¼-inch pieces. Add them to the bowl.

Cut the walnuts into ¼-inch pieces. Add them to the bowl.

Thoroughly mix all the ingredients, add the salad dressing and stir again. Serve immediately or refrigerate until needed.

Mom Tip

▼

Any crunchy raw vegetable
(carrots, cauliflower, red or green bell peppers, celery)
can be added to this dish, and any ingredient listed,
apart from the beans and salad dressing,
can be eliminated without changing
the taste too much. It's a good way
to clean out your vegetable bin.

Better-Than-the-Deli Four-Bean Salad

SERVES: 6-8

Preparation Time: 15 minutes ▼ Waiting Time: At least 3 hours
Cooking Time: None ▲ Rating: Very Easy

IF I WANTED ONLY ONE SERVING of bean salad, I'd probably just go to the deli. But I always want more, and I want it to taste like my mom's. Hers is sweeter than the store-bought variety, and it makes up to 15 servings. My mom says this dish goes with everything except spaghetti, but I always prefer to eat a big bowl of bean salad by itself. Luckily, it lasts for several weeks in the refrigerator.

It hardly seems like cooking when everything comes out of a can. I guess you could plant and grow the beans yourself if you are a real purist.

1	medium onion
¾	cup sugar
½	teaspoon black pepper
⅓	cup corn oil
⅓	cup vinegar (any kind)
1	15-ounce can red kidney beans
1	15-ounce can garbanzo beans (also called chick-peas)
1	15-ounce can green beans (cut or whole)
1	15-ounce can yellow wax beans

Peel and finely chop the onion and put in a large bowl. Add the sugar, black pepper, oil and vinegar and mix thoroughly.

Open the bean cans and drain and discard the liquid. Add all the beans to the bowl and mix thoroughly with the oil/vinegar dressing. Cover and refrigerate for several hours or overnight, stirring at least once, before serving (**see Mom Warning**). Consider the wait as equivalent to standing in a really long line at the deli.

Mom Tip

▼

You can vary the kind
of canned beans, adding
lima beans if you like, but
don't add beans with a sauce,
such as baked beans.

Mom Warning

▼

If you eat this salad
as soon as you make it,
the onions will be raw. They need
to soak in the dressing for several
hours to become "pickled."

Thai Pasta Salad

SERVES: 2-3 AS A MAIN COURSE

Preparation Time: 30 minutes ▼ **Cooking Time:** 20-30 minutes ▲ **Rating:** Not So Easy

THIS IS ONE OF MY FAVORITE RECIPES, and I have to convince you to make it even though it looks long and complicated. There's no one component that is taxing, but there are several things to do at once. Think of it as preparing a three-course meal of chicken, linguine and vegetables spiced with soy sauce and hoisin sauce. If you would like to feed a vegetarian this dish, don't add the chicken until you've served the vegetarian portion.

2	uncooked chicken breast halves (with bone or boneless; ¾-1 pound total)
1	9-ounce package fresh linguine or 8 ounces dried (see Mom Tip 1, page 72)
1	medium tomato
½	red bell pepper
10	sprigs fresh cilantro (see Mom Tip 2, page 72) or ¼ teaspoon ground coriander
1	garlic clove
¼	cup olive oil
¼	teaspoon red pepper flakes
3	tablespoons lemon juice
2	tablespoons soy sauce
2	tablespoons hoisin sauce (see Mom Tip 3, page 72)
½	teaspoon dried oregano
¼	teaspoon black pepper

Put the chicken in a small pot and cover with water. Bring to a boil over high heat, turn down the heat to medium and cook, covered, for 20 minutes. The chicken should be firm and white, with no signs of pink when you cut into it. If you see any pink juices, cook the chicken for another 5 minutes and test again. If you cook it too long, however, it will become tough.

Meanwhile, cover a large pot of water for cooking the pasta, and heat over high heat.

Transfer the chicken to a plate. Discard the cooking liquid. When the chicken has cooled enough to handle, pull off and discard the skin. Pull the meat from the bone (if there is one) and cut or tear it into bite-size strips. Put the chicken strips in a large serving bowl and set aside.

When the pasta water comes to a boil (about 10 minutes), cut or break the linguine into 4-inch lengths and add. Stir to make sure all the noodles are submerged. If you're using fresh linguine, set the timer for 3 minutes. If you're using dried, set the timer for 9 minutes. Stir occasionally to keep the noodles from clumping together. When the timer rings, taste a noodle to see if it's done. If it's a little too chewy, cook for another minute. When it's ready, turn off the heat and drain the noodles in a colander. Pour cold water over them to stop the cooking. Add the noodles to the bowl with the chicken.

Wash the tomato and cut it into ½-inch chunks. Wash the red bell pepper and cut it into ½-inch squares. Wash the cilantro sprigs, cut off and discard the stems and cut the leaves into ½-inch pieces (do not add the ground coriander now). Add these ingredients to the bowl.

To make the dressing, peel and finely chop the garlic. Heat the oil in a small pot. Add the garlic and the red pepper flakes and heat until the garlic begins to sizzle. Remove from the heat and add the lemon juice, soy sauce, hoisin sauce, oregano and black pepper. If you're using ground coriander instead of fresh cilantro, add it now.

Toss the salad, pour the dressing over it and toss again. Serve immediately or refrigerate until needed **(see Mom Warning)**. I prefer Thai Pasta Salad at room temperature.

Mom Tip 1
▼

Fresh linguine, a flattened spaghetti noodle, is available in the refrigerated section of many supermarkets. You can also buy it in Italian delicatessens. It costs more than dried, but it's well worth seeking out when making this salad because it tastes so much better cold.

Mom Tip 2
▼

Fresh cilantro has a larger leaf than fresh parsley. Like parsley, it is sold in bunches. It has a distinctive lemony taste and is a key ingredient in Mexican and Thai cooking. It will keep for about a week stored in a plastic bag in the vegetable bin. For longer storage, put the stem ends in a glass of water, cover with a plastic bag and refrigerate.

Mom Tip 3
▼

Hoisin sauce is a Chinese condiment, like ketchup, sold in jars in the specialty or Asian food section of the grocery store. You can also use sweet bean sauce, another Chinese condiment that tastes somewhat similar—a bit like plum jam but saltier.

Mom Warning
▼

If you have leftovers, be sure to store them in a covered container in the refrigerator. Otherwise, the noodles will dry out.

Chef's Salad

SERVES: 2 AS A MAIN COURSE

Preparation Time: 15 minutes ▼ Cooking Time: None ▲ Rating: Very Easy

Wʜᴀᴛ's ɪɴ ᴀ ᴄʜᴇꜰ's sᴀʟᴀᴅ? It depends on the chef. The first time I ordered it at a restaurant, I got a big bowl of lettuce, tomatoes and olives with some strips of ham and cheese. When I made it at home, I used up leftovers. I sure hope that's not what they did at the restaurant—at least not off somebody else's plate.

¼   head iceberg or leaf lettuce (see Mom Tip)
2   medium tomatoes
¼   pound cooked chicken or turkey (½ cup chopped)
¼   pound cooked ham or roast beef (½ cup chopped)
¼   pound Swiss cheese (½ cup shredded)
2   hard-cooked eggs, peeled
     Bottled salad dressing

Rinse the lettuce and tomatoes and pat dry with paper towels. Cut all the ingredients, except the dressing, into bite-size pieces, transfer them to a large salad bowl and toss thoroughly. Add your favorite salad dressing.

Mom Tip

▼

Many different types of lettuce are available to vary the look and flavor of this salad:
Bibb, Boston, endive, escarole, iceberg, red or green leaf, romaine. Fresh spinach is a good addition
to salads, but remove any straggly stems. All greens should be rinsed thoroughly in cold water,
except for iceberg, whose outer leaves alone need to be rinsed.

"Exploding Noodle" Chicken Salad

SERVES: 2-3 AS A MAIN COURSE

Preparation Time: 20 minutes (*if using already cooked chicken*)

or 45 minutes (*if using uncooked chicken*)

Cooking Time: 10 minutes ▲ Rating: Not So Easy

THIS IS A FANCY NAME for Chinese chicken salad, which combines cold chicken, lettuce and crispy noodles with an Asian dressing. Most of the recipe proceeds as a normal stir-fry would. But frying the rice sticks is the kitchen equivalent of fireworks. These seemingly mild-mannered noodles blow up to five times their original size in about two seconds. It's a spectacle worth witnessing, whether or not you plan to eat them.

½   head iceberg lettuce

1   cup cooked chicken or 2 uncooked chicken breast halves
      (with bone or boneless; ¾-1 pound total)

2   tablespoons corn oil or peanut oil + 2½-3 cups for frying rice sticks

3   tablespoons vinegar (any kind)

2   tablespoons sugar

1   tablespoon hoisin sauce (see Mom Tip 3 for Thai Pasta Salad, page 72)

2   teaspoons soy sauce

½   teaspoon dry mustard or 1½ teaspoons prepared mustard

½   teaspoon sesame oil (optional; see Mom Tip 1, page 76)

¼   7-ounce package rice sticks (see Mom Tip 2, page 76)

74

▼

Rinse the lettuce and pat dry with paper towels. Cut into ¼-inch shreds, up to 2 inches long, and transfer to a large salad bowl. If you're using cooked chicken, cut it into bite-size strips, add it to the bowl and set aside.

For uncooked chicken: Put the chicken in a small pot and cover with water. Bring to a boil over high heat. Turn down the heat to medium and cook, covered, for 20 minutes. The chicken should be firm and white, with no signs of pink when you cut into it. If you see any pink juices, cook the chicken for another 5 minutes and test again. If you cook it too long, however, it will become tough.

Transfer the chicken to a plate. Discard the cooking liquid. When the chicken has cooled enough to handle, pull off and discard the skin. Pull the meat from the bone (if there is one), cut or tear it into bite-size strips and add it to the bowl. Set aside.

Make the dressing by combining the 2 tablespoons oil, vinegar, sugar, hoisin sauce, soy sauce, mustard and sesame oil, if using, in a small bowl. Mix thoroughly and set aside.

Now it's time to deal with the rice sticks, which are really noodles made out of rice flour. They are very brittle and like to stick together in one big clump. Use about one-quarter of the package (see Mom Tip 2 for how to divide). Break or cut the noodles with scissors into two handfuls and try to separate them into small sections so the oil will reach them all equally during the frying process. Set aside.

Frying rice sticks will be a new experience for you. Pour the corn or peanut oil to a depth of ½ inch in a large wok, frying pan or pot and heat over medium-high heat. After about 2 minutes, test the oil to see if it's hot enough by dropping in a piece of rice stick. If it immediately puffs up and turns white, the oil is ready. If the rice stick just lies there, heat the oil for another minute. The biggest mistake you can make when frying rice sticks is not having the oil hot enough.

Have a spatula ready. When the oil is hot enough, drop in the first handful of rice sticks. They will immediately puff up (see Mom Warning). Turn them over and cook for a few seconds on the other side, pushing any unpuffed sticks into the oil. Drain the cooked rice sticks on paper towels. Then transfer them to the salad bowl.

Add more oil to the wok so that the oil is again ½ inch deep. As it heats, test it again. When it is hot enough, add the other handful of noodles, cook in the same manner and add them to the bowl. Cool the leftover oil, pour it into an empty can and discard it.

Toss the salad, pour the dressing on top and toss again. Serve immediately. Otherwise, the rice sticks will get soggy.

Mom Tip 1
▼

Sesame oil is an expensive, very flavorful oil that is available in the specialty or Asian food section of the grocery store.

Mom Tip 2
▼

Rice sticks are found in the specialty or Asian food section of the grocery store. Open the package of rice sticks inside a medium-size paper bag. The bag will keep the rice sticks from flying all over the room, especially when you break off a chunk. You can then store the leftover rice sticks in the paper bag.

Mom Warning
▼

Rice sticks burn quickly, so watch them constantly.

WALDORF SALAD

SERVES: 2-3

Preparation Time: 10 minutes ▼ Cooking Time: None ▲ Rating: Easy

THIS SALAD, SO I'M TOLD, is named after a New York hotel. Perhaps the resident chef had an odd assortment of leftovers and mixed them together. Celery, apples, walnuts and mayonnaise don't sound like they're made for each other, but somehow the combination works.

2 medium celery stalks
1 small apple or ½ large apple
½ cup walnut pieces
¼ cup mayonnaise

Wash the celery stalks, trim and discard the ends and cut the stalks into ¼-inch slices. Wash the apple but don't peel. Cut it in half and carve out and discard the core. Cut the apple into ½-inch pieces (**see Mom Warning**). Cut the walnut pieces into ¼-inch pieces.

Combine the celery, apple, walnuts and mayonnaise in a serving bowl and mix thoroughly. Serve immediately, or refrigerate until needed.

Mom Warning

▼

Peeled apples tend to turn brown when exposed to air, so don't
let the cut apple pieces sit around. Quickly mix them with the mayonnaise,
which will coat the surfaces and keep the apple white.

Potato Salad

SERVES: 4

Preparation Time: 25 minutes ▼ **Cooking Time:** 20 minutes ▲ **Rating:** Not So Easy

Everybody's mom has a different potato salad recipe. Potatoes are bland by nature, so the taste of potato salad depends on what else you put in it. This is the version I grew up with, so naturally I like it best.

1	pound potatoes (4-5 medium; see Mom Tip 1)
1	small onion
1	medium carrot
1	large celery stalk
2	radishes
½	cup sour cream
¼	cup mayonnaise
2	teaspoons sugar
2	teaspoons prepared mustard
2	teaspoons vinegar (any kind)
¼	teaspoon salt
⅛	teaspoon black pepper
⅛	teaspoon paprika
⅛	teaspoon garlic powder
⅛	teaspoon celery seeds

Peel the potatoes and cut them in half. Put them in a medium-size pot and cover with water. Bring to a boil over high heat. Once the water is boiling, turn down the heat to medium and cook, covered, for about

20 minutes, or until a sharp knife pushed through the potato meets no resistance (**see Mom Warning**). Check the potatoes occasionally and add extra water if there's less than an inch left.

While the potatoes are cooking, peel the onion and carrot and trim and discard ¼ inch from both ends of the carrot. Wash the celery stalk and radishes and trim and discard ¼ inch from each end. Hand-grate or chop the vegetables as fine as possible. If you're not up to that, simply cut them into bite-size pieces.

If you own a food processor, cut the vegetables into 2-inch pieces by hand and pulse them until they are finely chopped. If you have a blender, cut the vegetables into 2-inch pieces and fill the blender jar half-full. Add water to within 2 inches of the top of the blender. The water helps the vegetables circulate. Cover and blend so that the vegetables are finely chopped. Drain them thoroughly. Set the vegetables aside.

When the potatoes are cooked, drain, then cover them with cold water. When they are cool enough to handle, drain well. Cut them into ½-inch cubes and set aside.

Combine the sour cream, mayonnaise, sugar, mustard, vinegar, salt, black pepper, paprika, garlic powder and celery seeds in a large serving bowl. Stir thoroughly. Add the well-drained vegetable mixture and stir thoroughly. Add the potatoes and mix again.

Serve the potato salad immediately if you can't wait, or refrigerate overnight to let the flavor develop. It keeps for 3 to 4 days in the refrigerator but doesn't freeze well.

Mom Tip 1

▼

Any potatoes can be used,
but White Rose or red potatoes
hold their shape best. Russet potatoes
can get mushy, especially if they're
overcooked. But since russets
are the ones I usually have
around the house, I use them
anyway and no one complains.

Mom Tip 2

▼

Hard-cooked eggs
cut into eighths make a
good addition.

Mom Warning

▼

Don't let the water boil away.
Burned potatoes smell and
taste terrible, and the pot is
nearly impossible to clean.
So don't hesitate to add extra
water (boiling water,
if possible) midway
through cooking.

Fresh Fruit Salad

SERVES: 2

Preparation Time: 5-15 minutes, depending on fruit selection
Cooking Time: None ▼ Rating: Easy

FRUIT SALAD doesn't have to taste like it did in the school cafeteria. I don't think I'm the only person who has helped himself to tons of fruit salad because it looked so good, only to find that something has been done to it to make all the fruit taste the same. Maybe the key word here is "fresh."

Choose 4 or 5 fresh fruits from the following (see Mom Tip 1):

1	banana, peeled
1	small apple, unpeeled
1	peach, unpeeled
1	pear, unpeeled
1	plum, unpeeled
1	orange, peeled
1	kiwi, peeled (see Mom Tip 2)
12	grapes (seedless are best)
8	strawberries
8	cherries
½	grapefruit, peeled
½	cup blueberries
¼	cantaloupe or honeydew melon
1	slice watermelon

Wash and dry any fruit that doesn't need to be peeled (**see Mom Warning**). Cut away and discard melon rinds. Cut the grapefruit and orange in chunks. Remove any stems and large seeds. You don't want to stop midchew and spit out seeds. Cut your chosen fruits into bite-size pieces and combine them in a salad bowl.

Cover and refrigerate if you're not serving immediately, but bring the fruit salad back to room temperature before eating because the flavors will be stronger. There is no need for a dressing.

Mom Tip 1

▼

Be artistic.
Choose colors that
are eye-catching.
A few strawberries will
liven up the salad.

Mom Tip 2

▼

Kiwi is an egg-shaped fruit
with a brownish-green fuzzy skin.
The interior of the fruit is green with
small black seeds like a banana.
Peel the skin with a potato peeler
or a knife. Choose kiwis that
are just beginning to soften.
Underripe kiwis are as hard
as a rock and have little flavor.
Overripe kiwis are
soft and mushy.

Mom Warning

▼

Cut away bad spots
and avoid overripe fruit (mushy)
or underripe fruit (tasteless).

Sandwiches / Quesadillas / Pizzas

I THINK I HAD THE SAME THING FOR LUNCH from fourth grade through high school: tuna sandwiches. And I never got sick of them. I was like that dog in the "Far Side" cartoon with its tongue hanging out in anticipation, thinking, "Oh boy!

Dog food again!" I was never tempted to trade with my friends who were eager to give away their bologna, ham or (the worst) olive loaf sandwiches.

But now that I'm older, I'm willing to ease back on the tuna and switch to some of the other sandwiches in this section. But if I'm going to be cooking dinner, I don't want to spend a lot of time cooking lunch. So if a lunch recipe takes more than 15 minutes to make, I'm off to the deli. All of these are easy, fast and good, and none of them involves olive loaf.

Recipes

Croque Monsieur

SERVES: 1

Preparation Time: 2 minutes ▼ Cooking Time: 3-5 minutes ▲ Rating: Very Easy

CROQUE MONSIEUR sounds a lot more sophisticated than "ham sandwich." Actually, Croque Monsieur is the French name for "toasted ham and cheese sandwich." Of course, the French use French bread, not Wonder Bread. But even on pasty American sandwich bread, it's an easy way to get three food groups in a hurry.

  Butter or margarine
2 slices bread
1 slice Swiss cheese (see Mom Tip)
1 slice cooked ham

Butter 1 slice of bread and put it butter-side down in a small frying pan. Place the cheese on the bread and place the ham on the cheese. Butter the second slice of bread and place it butter side up on the ham.

Turn the heat to medium-high and cook the sandwich for 1 to 2 minutes per side, until both sides are golden brown and the cheese has melted. To speed the melting process, cover the frying pan. Be careful it doesn't burn. Serve immediately.

Mom Tip

▼

To vary the taste, substitute Cheddar or Muenster cheese.
The French also make a Croque Madame, which involves replacing
the ham with a slice of chicken or turkey.

Melted Cheese-Tuna Muffin

SERVES: 1

Preparation Time: 3 minutes (*if the tuna salad is already made*) or 8 minutes (*if the tuna is not made*)

Cooking Time: 2 minutes ▲ Rating: Very Easy

WHEN I WAS YOUNG AND DUMB, my mom often used this recipe as a bargaining tool. She would say, "Kevin, if you mow the lawn, I'll make you tuna and cheese on a muffin." I would rush out to the yard like a lab rat responding to a stimulus. Later I was disillusioned when I found out it was about the easiest dish in the world to make.

1	English muffin
½	cup Basic Tuna Salad (page 62)
2	slices Cheddar, Swiss or Monterey Jack cheese (see Mom Tip 1)

Preheat the broiler, with the top oven rack just under the broiling unit (**see Mom Tip 2**).

Cut an English muffin in half and toast each half in a toaster (**see Mom Warning**). Spread tuna salad on each half. Place a slice of cheese on top of the tuna. Place the muffins on a baking sheet, metal pie pan or broiling pan with a rack and put under the broiler.

Broil the muffins for 1 minute, or until the cheese melts. Watch them carefully. It seems like one microsecond after the cheese melts, it blackens. Serve immediately.

Mom Tip 1
▼

Use packaged sliced cheese or ¼-inch slices from a brick of cheese.

Mom Tip 2
▼

An alternative to broiling is oven-baking at 400 degrees for 2 minutes.

Mom Warning
▼

If you don't toast the English muffins first, they will be soggy.

Grilled Cheese-Tuna-Pickle Sandwich

SERVES: 1

Preparation Time: 3 minutes (*if the tuna salad is already made*) or 8 minutes (*if the tuna is not made*)
Cooking Time: 3-5 minutes ▼ **Rating:** Very Easy

I GREW UP EATING THIS SANDWICH. I always liked it because of the mixed-up flavors of tuna, melted cheese and pickles. A lot of delis give you a pickle seemingly as a decoration. I think I'm the only person who puts the pickle inside the sandwich. And a Grilled Cheese-Tuna-Pickle Sandwich is easy to make during a commercial.

1	teaspoon butter or margarine
2	slices bread
⅓	cup Basic Tuna Salad (page 62)
1	slice Cheddar or Monterey Jack cheese
1	small pickle or ½ large pickle

Melt the butter or margarine in a small frying pan over medium heat. As soon as it has melted, place 1 slice of bread in the pan. Spread the tuna salad over the bread. Add the cheese (**see Mom Tip**). Slice the pickle lengthwise into three thin slices and place them on top of the cheese. Add the second slice of bread, cover the pan and cook for 1 to 2 minutes, or until the cheese begins to melt and the bottom layer of bread is golden brown (**see Mom Warning**).

Remove the lid and carefully flip over the sandwich with a metal spatula. Cook for another 1 to 2 minutes, or until the new bottom layer has turned golden brown. Serve immediately.

Mom Tip

▼

If the cheese layer is in the middle, it will stick to the tuna salad and the pickle when it melts, making it easy to flip over the sandwich without having half the filling fall out.

Mom Warning

▼

If the heat is too high, the bottom layer of bread will burn before the cheese melts.

PITA PIZZA

SERVES: 1

Preparation Time: 5 minutes ▼ Cooking Time: 2 minutes ▲ Rating: Very Easy

WHEN I GO TO MY GRANDMA'S HOUSE, I'm used to getting three-course gourmet meals. So I was very surprised when she served me this makeshift excuse for pizza. But I kept asking for more. One weekend and three packages of pita bread later, she promised to give me my own toaster oven for Christmas so I could make Pita Pizza myself. In the meantime, I learned how to make it in a regular oven.

1	whole pita bread (6 inches in diameter)
4-6	tablespoons pizza sauce (see Mom Tip 1)
½	cup (2 ounces) shredded mozzarella cheese

Preheat the broiler. Make sure the top oven rack is in the highest position, just under the broiling unit (**see Mom Tip 2**).

Slice the pita bread around the circumference, separating it into 2 equal disks. Place them on a baking sheet, smooth side up, and broil for 30 seconds to crisp the bread.

Remove the baking sheet from the oven. Turn over the pita halves and spread 2 to 3 tablespoons pizza sauce on each, covering most of the surface. Sprinkle on the mozzarella cheese, dividing it between the pitas.

Return the baking sheet to the oven and broil for about 1 minute, or until the cheese melts. Keep the oven door open so that you can make sure the cheese doesn't burn (**see Mom Warning**). Serve hot.

Mom Tip 1

▼

If you don't have pizza sauce,
substitute tomato sauce mixed with
¼ teaspoon dried oregano,
¼ teaspoon dried basil and
¼ teaspoon garlic powder.

Mom Tip 2

▼

Pita Pizza is especially simple
to make in a toaster oven.
Follow the same directions
using the broiler setting.

Mom Warning

▼

"Broil" is not another word
for incinerate, but if you don't keep a
constant eye on your Pita Pizza, it
will become Pizza Toast or, even
worse, Charcoal Pita.

Spicy Potato Quesadillas

SERVES: 1-2

Preparation Time: 5 minutes ▼ Cooking Time: 7-8 minutes ▲ Rating: Easy

I TOOK FIVE YEARS OF SPANISH IN SCHOOL, yet the only words I seem to remember are "taco," "burrito," "nachos" and "quesadillas." To those not in the know, a quesadilla (kay-sah-DEE-ya) is a tortilla with melted cheese and other optional items. The optional items are what bulks this up from a snack to a meal. I used to store tortillas in the fridge, but they decayed faster than I could eat them. So now I keep them in the freezer, where they last for months.

1   medium potato

1   small onion

1   tablespoon corn oil

2   regular-size flour tortillas (about 7 inches in diameter; see Mom Tip 1)

½   cup (2 ounces) shredded Monterey Jack cheese

     Salsa

Peel the potato and cut it into ¼-inch cubes. Peel the onion and cut it into ¼-inch pieces.

Heat the oil in a medium-size frying pan over medium-high heat and when hot, add the potato and onion. Cook for 5 to 6 minutes, stirring frequently, until they begin to brown. Remove from the heat and set aside.

Put 1 tortilla in a clean, dry frying pan and begin heating over medium-high heat. When the tortilla is hot, less than 1 minute, turn it over and heat very briefly, no more than 30 seconds, on the other side (**see Mom Warning**). Heating takes away the raw taste of the tortilla.

Transfer the tortilla to a plate and spoon on half the cooked potato mixture and ¼ cup of the cheese. Add some salsa and fold or roll up the tortilla and eat. Repeat the procedure with the second tortilla.

Mom Tip 1

▼

There are two kinds of tortillas—
flour and corn. For this dish,
I prefer the taste of flour tortillas.
Corn tortillas are grittier.
They are more commonly used
for tacos and enchiladas.
However, they can be
used here.

Mom Tip 2

▼

The tortilla lends itself
to many fillings: black beans,
scrambled eggs, Basic Tuna Salad
(page 62) or leftover
vegetables sprinkled
with grated cheese.

Mom Warning

▼

Don't heat a tortilla
so long that it becomes brittle.
You need to be able to fold
it or roll it up to keep the
filling inside.

Not-Too-Messy Ham Barbecue

SERVES: 1-2

Preparation Time: 5 minutes ▼ Cooking Time: 3-5 minutes ▲ Rating: Very Easy

WHEN MOST PEOPLE think of barbecue, they think of cooking hamburgers or hot dogs on a backyard grill. This is the five-minute version, where you get to stay in the kitchen and not have to wait for the coals to get hot or worry about getting lighter fluid in your food. Because you're using a lot of the ingredients that make real barbecue, the flavor is almost like meat that has been grilled.

1   8-ounce can tomato sauce (see Mom Tip 1)
2   tablespoons sweet relish
1   tablespoon light or dark brown sugar
1½   teaspoons prepared mustard
1   teaspoon Worcestershire sauce
      Dash black pepper
½   pound cooked ham, very thinly sliced (see Mom Tip 2)
2   hamburger buns, toasted (see Mom Tip 3)

Combine the tomato sauce, relish, brown sugar, mustard, Worcestershire sauce, black pepper and ham in a medium-size pot. Stir thoroughly and bring to a boil over high heat. Turn down the heat to medium and cook, covered, for 2 minutes to heat through.

Cut the hamburger buns in half, fill each bun with half the ham and sauce and serve.

Mom Tip 1

▼

When you buy tomato sauce,
make sure you get the right can.
More than once, I've accidentally
picked up tomato paste or canned
tomatoes. They're right next
to each other on the shelf,
just to fool you.

Mom Tip 2

▼

If you buy ham at a deli or
the deli counter of a supermarket,
ask for it to be sliced very thin
(some regions of the country call
this chipped or shaved ham).
Packaged sliced ham is a little thick
for this recipe but will do in a
pinch. Thinly sliced turkey,
chicken or roast beef
can also be used.

Mom Tip 3

▼

If you toast the hamburger
buns while the barbecue mixture
is cooking, they won't get
soggy so fast.

Really Sloppy Joes

SERVES: 4 NORMAL PEOPLE, OR 2 VERY HUNGRY PEOPLE

Preparation Time: 5 minutes ▼ Cooking Time: 25 minutes ▲ Rating: Easy

I LIKE Sloppy Joes because they have more flavor than a hamburger. When I first tried this recipe, I poured the fat into the sink. That made perfect sense to me; it was a liquid. Unfortunately, the fat solidified in the drain, and we had to call the plumber before we could wash dishes again. Now I pour the fat into an empty can, but there is potential for disaster here as well, as I explain in Spaghetti Bolognese (page 101).

1	pound lean ground beef (see Mom Tip 1)
1	medium onion
⅔	cup ketchup
¼	cup water
1	tablespoon vinegar (any kind)
1	teaspoon Worcestershire sauce
1	teaspoon prepared mustard
¼	teaspoon garlic powder
6	drops hot pepper sauce
4	hamburger buns, toasted (see Mom Tip 2)

Brown the beef in a large frying pan over medium-high heat for about 10 minutes, stirring frequently at first to break the meat into small clumps. If the beef seems like it's starting to burn, turn the heat down to medium. It's not necessary to add oil since even the leanest beef has fat in it. Carefully drain the fat into an empty can and discard.

While the beef is browning, peel the onion and chop it into ¼-inch pieces. After the fat has been drained off, add the onion to the beef. Cook for 2 minutes, stirring frequently.

Add the ketchup, water, vinegar, Worcestershire sauce, mustard, garlic powder and hot pepper sauce and cook, uncovered, over medium-low heat, stirring occasionally, for 10 minutes. Add up to ¼ cup more water if the mixture seems too dry. It should be thick and juicy rather than watery.

Spoon one-quarter of the mixture into each bun half, top with the other half and serve like a burger. Or, if you don't want to get your hands sloppy, open the buns flat and spoon one-eighth of the mixture on each bun half and eat with a fork. Repeat with the remaining buns.

Mom Tip 1

▼

The amount of fat
in ground beef varies from less
than 7 percent to at least 30 percent.
The leaner the beef, the higher
the price, but the less fat you'll
be draining off.

Mom Tip 2

▼

If you toast the hamburger
buns while the Sloppy Joe mixture
is cooking, they won't get
soggy so fast.

Overstuffed Calzones

SERVES: 2

Preparation Time: 30 minutes ▼ Waiting Time: 4 hours (*if the dough has not been previously thawed*)

Cooking Time: 15-18 minutes ▲ Rating: Not So Easy

I NEVER HEARD THE WORD "CALZONE" until I went to college. My new friends complained that they couldn't wait to get back to New York City to get a decent calzone. Not wanting to appear ignorant, I said, "Yeah, nothing like a good calzone." To me, a calzone could have been a kind of massage. I learned the truth a few months later when I went to New York City and saw somebody eating what looked like a huge apple turnover. It turned out to be a calzone, which I now know to be a filling-on-the-inside pizza.

1	1-pound loaf frozen bread dough (see Mom Tip)
1½	teaspoons olive oil
4	medium mushrooms
1	small onion
1	garlic clove
¼	red bell pepper
¼	cup flour
1	6-ounce can Italian tomato paste or ½ cup pizza sauce
¼	cup sliced pepperoni (optional)
1	cup (4 ounces) shredded mozzarella cheese
2	teaspoons grated Parmesan cheese

Put the frozen bread dough in an oiled bowl and let it sit out, covered, at room temperature for 4 hours. When the bread doubles in size, it is ready.

Preheat the oven to 400 degrees. Grease a baking sheet with ½ teaspoon of the oil and set aside.

To make the filling, wash the mushrooms and cut away and discard the bottom ¼ inch of the stems. Slice the mushrooms thin. Peel and finely chop the onion and garlic. Cut the red bell pepper into ¼-inch pieces. Set aside.

The dough will be sticky, so add 1 tablespoon of the flour and work it into the dough with your hands. Continue adding more flour, a tablespoon at a time (up to ¼ cup), until the dough is no longer sticky. Divide the dough in half.

Flatten out 1 piece of dough into a large (10-inch) circle on the greased baking sheet. I use a combination of my hands and the side of a vinegar bottle, although any cylindrical shape will do. Cover the dough with half the tomato paste or pizza sauce, leaving 1 inch bare all around the circumference. Then add half of the mushrooms, onion, garlic, red bell pepper, pepperoni, mozzarella and Parmesan cheese.

Fold the dough circle in half, enclosing the stuffing. Tightly press the edges of the dough together with your fingers, creating a fat half-moon shape. The fatter the better, because the filling will shrink as it cooks. Slide the calzone to one side of the baking sheet. Flatten out the other dough circle on the remaining surface of the baking sheet, cover with the remaining ingredients, and fold the circle over as before.

Lightly spread the remaining 1 teaspoon olive oil on the top of the calzones and bake, without turning, for 15 to 18 minutes, or until the dough puffs up and turns brown. Check the progress during the last few minutes of baking so the calzones don't burn. Serve hot or cooled.

Mom Tip

▼

Frozen bread dough is sold in 3-pound packages,
with each 1-pound loaf individually wrapped. To eliminate the waiting time,
the dough can be thawed overnight in the refrigerator. Remove it from the
refrigerator 1 hour before you're ready to use it so that it will reach
room temperature. Then add flour as directed.

PASTA

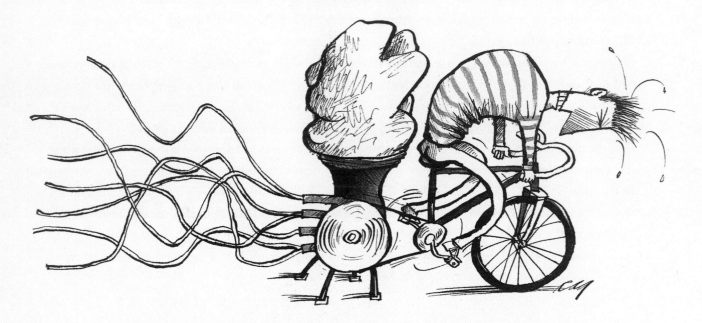

PASTA IS ONE OF THE FEW FOODS that vegetarians and nonvegetarians can enjoy equally. Thank goodness. Otherwise my girlfriend and I would eat together far less often. While I love meat, particularly Spaghetti Bolognese, it's Spaghetti with Pesto Sauce more than anything that has kept our romance going.

I'm no yuppie, and neither is she. We don't even drink latte. But I did buy her a pastamaker for her birthday. It turned out to be more of a dual-purpose pasta-maker/exercise machine. Together we stood in the kitchen and braced ourselves as we tried to turn the crank. Eventually a few noodles squirted out the other side. It did taste good, but not good enough to get a hernia over. And besides, who wants to have linguine draped over every chair and hanging on every towel rack to dry? That's why you won't find a recipe for fresh pasta in here.

It's been said that eating pasta can give you extra energy. My dad "carbo-loads" the night before he runs a 10K race. He eats six plates of Linguine with Clam Sauce. Strangely it doesn't improve his time. As for me, I don't run. I do carbo-load, though—whenever I know I'll have to use the pastamaker.

Recipes

How to Cook Pasta

FILL A LARGE POT AT LEAST HALF FULL of hot tap water, cover and begin heating over high heat. When the water comes to a boil, add the noodles, a handful at a time, and stir to make sure they are submerged. Check the package to see how long the pasta should cook and set the timer accordingly. Then stir every minute or two to keep the noodles from sticking together. When the buzzer rings, taste a strand to see if it's soft enough. If it is, turn off the heat and drain the noodles in a colander or strainer. If it isn't, cook for another minute.

For reference, 4 ounces dried pasta equals 2 to 2½ cups cooked pasta. Some cooks serve 4 ounces dried pasta per person. I like larger portions, so I allow 5 ounces. Pasta is cheap, and it's always good left over. Besides, if you need to cook more at the last minute, it will take at least 15 minutes, assuming you have to boil more water.

If you don't have a kitchen scale, here is a good way to calculate 5 ounces of dried spaghetti: Crook your index finger and your thumb in a circle the size of a quarter. Fill the circle with vertical strands of uncooked spaghetti. This is approximately 5 ounces. Fresh pasta comes in 9-ounce packages. Each package will provide 2 hearty portions.

Speaking of fresh pasta, you may wonder what its advantages are since it costs three or four times as much as dried. It tastes good—some think better than dried pasta. It takes only 2 to 3 minutes to cook once the water is boiling. And you can keep packages of it in the freezer. Try it and decide for yourself.

If the pasta is ready before the sauce, drain it and put it back in the pot. Add 1 tablespoon oil, mix thoroughly and cover. The oil will help prevent the noodles from sticking together.

Spaghetti Bolognese

SERVES: 3-4

Preparation Time: 20 minutes ▼ **Cooking Time:** 45-50 minutes ▲ **Rating:** Easy

WHEN I WAS GROWING UP, we used to have Spaghetti Bolognese (spaghetti with meat sauce) once a week. I thought it was the only way you could have spaghetti. Then my dad started making Linguine with Clam Sauce. Not to be outdone, my mom began experimenting with other sauces. Still I find myself making Spaghetti Bolognese once a week.

My first attempt, however, almost caused me to stop cooking altogether. I decided to drain every ounce of fat into an empty can. I kept tipping the pan until the meat was upside down, with only a lid between the beef and gravity. I began to shake the pan. Bad move! Within seconds, the lid had slipped and the meat was all over the floor. I stood over the mess, stunned. I sulked for awhile, and then I ordered a pizza. I didn't clean it up until the next day.

My three pieces of advice to you on draining fat: (1) Use a proper pot lid with a heatproof handle; (2) tip the pan just a little more than 90 degrees—not 180 degrees—when you're pouring off the fat into an empty can; (3) use a tablespoon to spoon out the last remaining fat droplets.

1	medium onion
1	garlic clove
¼	pound fresh mushrooms or an 8-ounce can mushrooms
2	large celery stalks
1	pound lean ground beef
1	tablespoon sugar
½	teaspoon dried oregano
½	teaspoon dried parsley

½   teaspoon salt

¼   teaspoon black pepper

1   12-ounce can tomato paste + 1 can water

16   ounces spaghetti

To make the sauce, peel and finely chop the onion and garlic. Wash the fresh mushrooms, cut away and discard the bottom ¼ inch of the stems, and slice the mushrooms thin. Or open the can of mushrooms and discard the liquid. Wash the celery stalks, trim and discard the ends and cut the stalks into ¼-inch slices. Set the vegetables aside.

Without adding oil, brown the beef in a frying pan or medium-size pot over medium heat, stirring frequently to break the meat into small clumps. This process takes about 10 minutes. After the meat has browned, drain any fat by covering the pan with a lid and carefully pouring the liquid into an empty can. Throw away the can.

Meanwhile, cover a large pot of water and begin heating it over medium-low heat. You won't need to add the noodles for about 30 minutes, but at least the water will be ready.

Add the onion, garlic, mushrooms, celery, sugar, oregano, parsley, salt, black pepper, tomato paste and water to the meat mixture. Stir thoroughly. Cook, covered, over low heat for 30 minutes. Stir every 10 minutes and add up to ½ cup more water if the sauce seems too thick (**see Mom Warning**). I like my sauce thick, but some may prefer it thinner.

When the sauce has finished cooking, add the spaghetti to the boiling water and stir to make sure all the noodles are submerged. Turn up the heat to medium-high and set the timer for 8 minutes for dried pasta, 3 minutes for fresh. Continue to stir every minute or two to keep the noodles from sticking together. When the timer rings, taste a noodle to see if it's done. If it's a little too chewy, cook for another minute. Drain the noodles in a colander in the sink.

Transfer the noodles to a large serving bowl and top with the meat sauce. Serve at once.

Mom Tip

▼

If you have too much
spaghetti and too little sauce,
you can extend the sauce by adding
more water or an 8-ounce can
of tomato sauce.

Mom Warning

▼

If the heat is too high,
the sauce will stick to the
bottom and burn.

Spaghetti with Pesto Sauce

SERVES: 2

Preparation Time: 10 minutes ▼ **Cooking Time:** None (*sauce*), 8 minutes (*spaghetti*)

Rating: Very Easy (*with a food processor or blender*)

In an attempt to convince me that vegetarians eat as well as anyone else, my girlfriend cooked Spaghetti with Pesto Sauce for me. She was in seventh heaven, but at first, I was stuck in fourth or fifth. Since that time, I've come to appreciate how a sticky green paste can replace ground beef. And it's really easy to make if you have a blender or food processor. Don't try it unless you have one. I just have one complaint: Why do pine nuts cost so much?

2	garlic cloves
1	cup loosely packed fresh basil leaves (see Mom Tip 1)
2	tablespoons pine nuts or walnuts (see Mom Tip 2)
⅓	cup olive oil
¼	cup grated Parmesan cheese
¼	teaspoon black pepper
	Dash salt
10	ounces spaghetti

Cover a large pot of water and begin heating over high heat. While you're waiting for it to boil (about 10 minutes), make the Pesto Sauce.

Peel the garlic. Put the garlic, basil leaves and pine nuts or walnuts in the bowl of a food processor or blender and chop until they are as smooth as possible. With the machine on, add the olive oil in a slow but steady stream. Add the Parmesan cheese, black pepper and salt and blend just until mixed. Transfer the sauce to a small bowl and set aside. This sauce does not need to be cooked.

When the water comes to a boil, add the spaghetti. Stir to make sure all the noodles are submerged. Set the timer for 8 minutes for dried pasta, 3 minutes for fresh. Continue to stir every minute or two to keep the noodles from sticking together. When the timer rings, taste a noodle to see if it's done. If it's a little too chewy, cook for another minute. Drain the noodles in a colander in the sink. Transfer the noodles to a large serving bowl and pour on the Pesto Sauce. Stir and serve.

Mom Tip 1

▼

Fresh basil is available
in small packages in the
vegetable section of most
grocery stores.

Mom Tip 2

▼

Pine nuts, which are actually
seeds from certain pine trees, may
be a little hard to find. If they're not
available in the Italian, nut or specialty
food sections of your supermarket,
try a deli. Or substitute walnuts,
which taste nearly the same.
Ready-made pesto sauce is
available in some stores.

Linguine with Clam Sauce

SERVES: 2

Preparation Time: 10 minutes ▼ Cooking Time: 25 minutes ▲ Rating: Very Easy

THIS IS THE ONE MEAL MY DAD CAN COOK. When my mom was out of town, we would have this dish every night. So when I feel nostalgic for those old male-bonding times, I get out this recipe.

1	medium onion
5	garlic cloves
2	tablespoons olive oil
1	tablespoon dried parsley
	Dash black pepper
1	15-ounce can ready-cut tomatoes (see Mom Tip 2 for Bacon and Tomato Soup, page 41)
1	6-ounce can chopped or minced baby clams
10	ounces linguine (see Mom Tip)

Cover a large pot of water and begin heating over medium-low heat. You won't need to add the noodles for about 20 minutes, but at least the water will be ready. Meanwhile, make the sauce.

Peel and finely chop the onion and garlic. Heat the oil in a large frying pan over medium heat. Add the onion, garlic, parsley and black pepper and cook for about 5 minutes, stirring occasionally, until the onion begins to soften. Add the tomatoes and their liquid and the clam juice from the clams. Save the clams to add later (see **Mom Warning**).

Cook, uncovered, over medium-low heat for 20 minutes, stirring occasionally. The mixture should bubble but not boil energetically. The sauce will gradually thicken as the liquid evaporates. Be careful that all the liquid doesn't boil away. Add up to ¼ cup water if the tomato pieces aren't surrounded by any sauce.

After the sauce has cooked for 10 minutes, add the linguine to the boiling water. Stir to make sure all the noodles are submerged. Turn up the heat and set the timer for 8 minutes for dried pasta, 3 minutes for fresh. Continue to stir every minute or two to keep the noodles from sticking together. When the timer rings, taste a noodle to see if it's done. If it's a little too chewy, cook for another minute. Drain the noodles in a colander in the sink.

While the cooked noodles are draining, add the clams to the sauce, turn up the heat to medium-high and cook for 1 minute to heat the clams, which are already cooked. Transfer the noodles to a large serving bowl and top with the clam sauce. Serve at once.

Mom Tip
▼

Linguine is a flattened
spaghetti noodle about ¼ inch
wide. Regular spaghetti can be
substituted.

Mom Warning
▼

Clams get tough
if cooked a long time, so add
them only at the end.

Sizzling Pork Noodles

SERVES: 3

Preparation Time: 15 minutes ▼ Cooking Time: 20 minutes ▲ Rating: Very Easy

I USED TO ASK MY MOM to make this Chinese-style spaghetti when I came home for vacations. I was tired of pizza and Chinese take-out. Now that I'm on my own, I cook it and leave it in a big bowl in the refrigerator (covered, of course) and reheat it for three or four meals. Vermicelli or angel hair pasta—two fancy names for thin noodles—are especially good with this sauce. I love soy sauce, which makes this dish taste like hot-and-sour spaghetti. You can adjust the amount of soy to your taste. The cucumber and scallions provide a surprising contrast and crunch.

1	medium onion
2	garlic cloves
1	pound lean ground pork
½	cup chili sauce (or 7 tablespoons ketchup + 1 tablespoon bottled horseradish)
¼	cup water
3	tablespoons soy sauce
1	tablespoon vinegar (any kind)
¼	teaspoon black pepper
12	ounces vermicelli
½	large cucumber
2	scallions

Cover a large pot of water and begin heating it over high heat (**see Mom Tip**). While you're waiting for it to boil (about 10 minutes), make the sauce.

Peel and finely chop the onion and garlic and set aside. Without using oil, brown the pork in a frying pan over medium heat, stirring frequently to break the meat into small clumps. This process takes about 10 minutes. After the meat has browned, drain any fat by covering the pan with a lid and carefully pouring the liquid into an empty can. Throw away the can.

Add the onion, garlic, chili sauce (or ketchup and horseradish), water, soy sauce, vinegar and black pepper to the pan and stir. Cook, uncovered, over medium heat, stirring occasionally for about 8 minutes, or until most of the liquid has evaporated. Turn off the heat and cover to keep hot.

Once the sauce is cooking, add the vermicelli to the boiling water and stir to make sure all the noodles are submerged. Set the timer for 7 minutes for dried pasta, 2 minutes for fresh. Continue to stir every minute or two to keep the noodles from sticking together. When the timer rings, taste a noodle to see if it's done. If it's a little too chewy, cook for another minute. Drain the noodles in a colander in the sink.

While the noodles are cooking, peel the cucumber and cut it into ¼-inch cubes. Wash the scallions. Cut off the root tips and top 2 inches of the green ends and discard them. Cut the remaining white and green parts into ¼-inch pieces and set aside.

When the noodles are done, drain them and transfer to a large bowl or platter. Pour the pork sauce on top. Sprinkle with the cucumber and scallion pieces and serve.

Mom Tip

▼

If you use hot water instead of cold water
when you start heating the water for the noodles,
it will come to a boil more quickly.

Spaghetti with Spinach and Mushrooms

SERVES: 2

Preparation Time: 15 minutes ▼ Cooking Time: 25-30 minutes ▲ Rating: Easy

I STARTED OUT MAKING SPAGHETTI with garlic sauce, but it was tasteless. My girlfriend suggested adding spinach, so I bought a fresh bunch. I regretted it after spending an hour cleaning off all that sand and grit in the leaves. My mom informed me that frozen spinach is precleaned and sent me this recipe.

1	10-ounce package frozen leaf spinach (see Mom Tip)
½	pound medium mushrooms
3	garlic cloves
1	tablespoon olive oil
1	tablespoon butter or margarine
3	tablespoons lemon juice
	Dash black pepper
	Dash salt
½	cup whipping (not whipped) cream (see Mom Tip for Crustless Quiche, page 123)
10	ounces spaghetti
	Grated Parmesan cheese

Cover a large pot of water and begin heating over medium heat. You'll need it in about 15 minutes. Meanwhile, start making the sauce.

Cook the spinach according to the package directions (about 6 minutes), drain and set aside. Wash the mushrooms and cut away and discard the bottom ¼ inch of the stems. Slice the mushrooms thin and set aside.

Peel and finely chop the garlic. Heat the oil and butter or margarine in a small frying pan over medium-high heat. Add the garlic and cook, stirring frequently, for 1 minute. Add the mushrooms and cook, stirring occasionally, for 2 minutes. Add the lemon juice, black pepper, salt and cream; stir again. Set aside.

When the water comes to a boil, add the spaghetti. Stir to make sure all the noodles are submerged. Turn up the heat and set the timer for 8 minutes for dried pasta, 3 minutes for fresh. Continue to stir every minute or two to keep the noodles from sticking together. When the timer rings, taste a noodle to see if it's done. If it's a little too chewy, cook for another minute. Drain the noodles in a colander in the sink.

Reheat the mushroom sauce until it is hot but not boiling. Add the cooked spinach to the now empty spaghetti pot. When the sauce is hot, add it to the spinach and mix thoroughly. Add the drained spaghetti to the pot and mix again. Sprinkle with Parmesan cheese and serve.

Mom Tip

▼

Fresh spinach would probably taste better,
but cleaning it may take more time than cooking the whole dish.
If you feel inspired, put the spinach in a large pot, fill with water and swish
the leaves around in the water. Most of the grit will sink to the bottom.
Lift the leaves out of the water and rinse each one in cold running
water to remove any remaining grit. I compromise and use
frozen spinach and fresh mushrooms.

Eggs / Cheese

I CALL THIS THE CHOLESTEROL SECTION. I have a friend who says that cholesterol can only hurt you if you believe in it. He's no nutritionist, but it sounds like a reasonable theory to me. Of course, I wouldn't trade arteries with him.

Let's face it: I like eggs. I like to fry and scramble them. I haven't yet tried drinking them raw like Rocky, but I'm not afraid to eat quiche. My refrigerator might be close to empty some days, but one thing is never missing—eggs.

When we go shopping, my girlfriend makes fun of me for opening all of the boxes to find the most perfect eggs. But then she spends half an hour examining the milk cartons, trying to find the one with the latest expiration date. Don't ask me about our forays into the cheese department.

Recipes

French Toast

SERVES: 1

Preparation Time: 3 minutes ▼ Cooking Time: 3-4 minutes ▲ Rating: Very Easy

EVERY TIME I BUY BREAD, half the loaf gets stale. Instead of feeding the pigeons, I whip up a batch of French Toast. Amending the old saying, a bird in the park is worth two pieces of French Toast in my apartment. If the bread is green, however, feed it to the garbage disposal.

- 1   large egg
- 1½   tablespoons corn oil
- 2   slices bread (stale preferred)
      Maple syrup (see Mom Tip 1)

Beat the egg in a soup bowl large enough to accommodate a slice of bread, but don't put in the bread yet.

Heat the oil in a large frying pan over medium-high heat. While it's heating, dip a slice of bread into the beaten egg, turn it over to coat the second side and carefully place it in the pan. Do all this quickly so that the first slice doesn't have a chance to absorb all the egg. Because stale bread is drier, it won't become as mushy (see Mom Tip 2). Repeat the procedure with the second slice of bread and add it to the pan.

Cook for about 2 minutes. Lift the bread partway with a spatula to see how it's cooking. When the bread has browned on one side, turn it over and cook it for 1 to 2 minutes, or until the other side has browned. Serve immediately with syrup.

Mom Tip 1

▼

If you don't have any syrup,
sprinkle the French Toast with
1 teaspoon sugar mixed with
⅛ teaspoon cinnamon.

Mom Tip 2

▼

If there's not quite enough
egg left to fully coat the second slice
of bread, add 1 tablespoon milk and
beat it into the remaining egg.
However, too much milk
makes the French
Toast mushy.

Pancakes from Scratch

SERVES: 2

Preparation Time: 5 minutes ▼ Cooking Time: 5-10 minutes ▲ Rating: Easy

I USED TO THINK USING BISQUICK was the only way to make pancakes. So I was incredulous when my girlfriend offered to make pancakes for me when I knew we were out of Bisquick. As she was mixing up the ingredients, I kept saying, "This is going to taste terrible." I wasn't shocked that they turned out well— I'm a bit more stable than that—but I was pleasantly surprised. Now there's one less large box I have to find a place for in my cupboard.

1	cup flour
1	tablespoon sugar
1	teaspoon baking powder
½	teaspoon salt
1	cup milk
1	large egg
2	tablespoons butter or margarine, melted
1	tablespoon corn oil, plus more as needed
	Butter
	Maple syrup

Combine the flour, sugar, baking powder and salt in a large bowl. Add the milk, egg and melted butter or margarine and mix until combined (**see Mom Tip 1**).

Heat the oil in a large frying pan or griddle over medium-high heat. After the oil has heated for 1 minute, flick a drop of water into the pan. If it immediately sizzles, it's time to cook the pancakes.

Small pancakes are easier to cook and turn over, so using about ¼ cup batter per pancake, pour 3 to 4 pancakes into the pan. Cook for about 2 minutes, or until the bubbles that appear on the surface of the pancakes begin to break. After 1 minute, lift the edge of 1 pancake to make sure the bottom isn't getting too brown. If it is, reduce the heat to medium. Flip the pancakes over with a spatula and cook them for 1 more minute. The second side will not get as uniformly brown.

Serve this first batch with butter and syrup and immediately start on the second batch. You shouldn't need additional oil in the pan, but if the batter starts to stick, add 1 more tablespoon oil to the pan.

Mom Tip 1

▼

When you're mixing the batter,
don't worry about any lumps.
They disappear during
cooking.

Mom Tip 2

▼

To make blueberry pancakes,
add ½ cup blueberries
to the batter.

Vegetable Omelet

SERVES: 2

Preparation Time: 10 minutes ▼ Cooking Time: 15-20 minutes ▲ Rating: Easy

SOME SAY THAT MAKING OMELETS is an art form. Here's the finger-painting version.

1	large potato
1	medium onion
1	garlic clove
4	medium mushrooms
2	tablespoons butter or margarine
4	large eggs
2	tablespoons water
	Dash salt
	Dash black pepper
	Salsa

Preheat the broiler. Make sure the top oven rack is in the highest position, just under the broiling unit.

Peel and cut the potato into ¼-inch cubes. Peel the onion and chop it into ¼-inch pieces. Peel and finely chop the garlic. Wash the mushrooms and cut away and discard the bottom ¼ inch of the stems. Slice the mushrooms thin.

Melt the butter or margarine in a large ovenproof frying pan over medium heat. Add the potato and cook, stirring occasionally, for 3 minutes. Add the onion, garlic and mushrooms and cook, stirring occasionally, for 2 minutes. The vegetables will begin to soften.

While the vegetables cook, break the eggs in a bowl, add the water, salt and black pepper and beat until frothy. Pour the eggs into the pan, cover, turn the heat to low and cook for about 10 minutes, or until the eggs are set, which means they're no longer runny. However, they will appear uncooked on top.

Remove the lid from the frying pan and put the pan under the broiler, with the handle sticking out and the oven door open. Broil the eggs for about 1 minute, or until the top surface begins to brown. Serve immediately with salsa.

Mom Tip

▼

You can add a variety of vegetables to this dish:
broccoli, celery, red and green bell peppers, zucchini. Just be sure
to cut them into ¼-inch pieces and cook them as you're cooking the potato.
You also can sprinkle on some shredded Cheddar or Monterey Jack
cheese just before putting the omelet under the broiler.

Brunch Burrito

SERVES: 1

Preparation Time: 10 minutes ▼ Cooking Time: 10 minutes ▲ Rating: Easy

WHEN I OVERSLEEP, I know something's got to give if I want to get to work or school on time. Either I don't shower, don't eat or don't dress. Given that choice, I usually don't eat—or didn't until my mom told me about Brunch Burritos. In her other job as a film journalist, she had noticed movie hands walking around sets carrying these Mexican-style egg sandwiches. She used her investigative skills to get the recipe and then sent it to me. I admit that downing a bowl of cereal is quicker and less messy, but I found that a Brunch Burrito tastes better, is a lot more filling and can be eaten while you're racing off.

2	large eggs
2	tablespoons water
	Dash salt
	Dash black pepper
2	"burrito-size" flour tortillas (10-12 inches in diameter)
1	tablespoon canned green chilies (not canned jalapeño peppers)
	Handful shredded Cheddar or Monterey Jack cheese
½	small onion
2	teaspoons butter or margarine
	Salsa

Break the eggs into a bowl, add the water, salt and black pepper and beat.

Place the tortillas, one on top of the other, on a serving plate and set aside. (You use 2 tortillas so the filling doesn't drip through.) Have the chilies and cheese ready.

Peel the onion and chop it into small pieces. Melt 1 teaspoon of the butter or margarine in a medium-size frying pan over medium-high heat. Add the onion and cook for about 5 minutes, stirring occasionally, until the onion begins to soften. Remove the onion from the pan and set aside.

Add the remaining 1 teaspoon butter or margarine to the pan. When it has melted and is frothy, add the egg mixture and let it set for about 2 minutes over medium-high heat (**see Mom Warning**). Don't scramble. As the egg cooks, lift it gently with a spatula so that the uncooked mixture can flow underneath. Tip the pan if necessary. When the egg is no longer runny, flip it over with the spatula.

Sprinkle on the onion, chilies and cheese and cover for about 30 seconds to allow the cheese to begin to melt. Slide the cooked egg out of the pan, tipping the pan and using the spatula to ease it onto the double tortilla. Add as much salsa as you like and roll up the tortillas together into a package, tucking in the ends. Serve with a bunch of napkins.

Mom Tip

▼

Crumbled bacon
and sliced mushrooms
(cooked along with the onion)
make good additions
to this burrito.

Mom Warning

▼

To keep from burning the eggs,
be aware of the thickness of the frying
pan. If it's made of cast iron or is
very heavy, use medium-high or
high heat. If it's thin,
use low heat.

Crustless Quiche

SERVES: 2

Preparation Time: 10 minutes

Cooking Time: 35-40 minutes ▼ **Rating:** Very Easy

MY FRIEND SCOTT ridicules quiche, calling it "egg pie." But he still lives at home, so his opinion doesn't count. As a matter of fact, quiche is a lot more than egg pie. It has bacon, cream, spices . . . and eggs. I'm not interested in my reputation in the world of real men who don't eat quiche. I like it because it's very easy to make. The lack of a crust makes this quiche look like an amoeba, but it's much easier that way.

1	teaspoon corn oil
2	tablespoons dry bread crumbs
4	slices bacon
3	large eggs
1	cup whipping (not whipped) cream (see Mom Tip)
⅛	teaspoon ground nutmeg
⅛	teaspoon salt
⅛	teaspoon black pepper

Preheat the oven to 375 degrees.

Add the oil to an 8- or 9-inch pie pan to prevent the quiche from sticking, and spread it around with a piece of paper towel, making sure to oil the sides as well as the bottom. Sprinkle the bread crumbs into the pan and swish them around until they cling to all the oiled surfaces. Leave any extra crumbs in the bottom. Set aside.

Put the bacon in a large frying pan and begin heating over medium-high heat. As the bacon cooks, it will begin to shrink. After 2 to 3 minutes, you may want to drain off the fat into an empty can. After the bacon browns on one side, turn it over and cook until it gets crisp, about 2 minutes. Turn down the heat to medium so that it doesn't burn (**see Mom Warning**). Drain the bacon for several minutes on paper towels, patting the tops with another paper towel. Break or cut the slices into 1-inch pieces.

Combine the bacon, eggs, cream, nutmeg, salt and black pepper in a medium-size bowl and beat thoroughly. Pour the mixture into the pie pan and bake for 25 to 30 minutes, or until the quiche puffs up and begins to brown. A knife inserted in the center should come out clean. Let cool for 5 to 10 minutes and serve.

Mom Tip

▼

Whipping cream,
located near the milk at the
grocery store, is available in
½-pint (1-cup) and
1-pint portions.

Mom Warning

▼

Old bacon is more apt
to burn than fresh bacon. If you
can't use an entire package within
a few days, wrap part of it
in aluminum foil and
freeze it.

Egg Salad with Dill and Mustard

SERVES: 2-3 AS A SALAD OR SANDWICH FILLING

Preparation Time: 10 minutes ▼ Cooking Time: 20 minutes ▲ Rating: Very Easy

Hard-cooking eggs is an act of faith because there's no way to know if they're done without cracking them open or using an X-ray machine. Occasionally I'll start peeling one and find that it's still runny. Other times the yolk has turned green, which means I cooked it way too long. What I do now is just follow the foolproof formula described here.

This egg salad is different from the garden-variety one because my mom had to use spices to disguise the mayonnaise, which my dad refuses to eat. To this day, he doesn't believe egg salad has mayonnaise in it.

4	large eggs
1	scallion
1	small celery stalk
3	tablespoons mayonnaise
2	tablespoons sour cream
1	teaspoon dried dill (see Mom Tip 1)
1	teaspoon prepared mustard
	Dash salt
	Dash black pepper

Gently place the eggs in a medium-size pot, cover with water and bring the water to a boil over high heat. As soon as the water begins to boil, turn down the heat to medium and cook, covered, for 3 minutes (**see Mom Tip 2 and Mom Warning**). Turn off the heat and let the eggs sit in the hot water, covered, for 15 minutes.

While the eggs are cooking, wash the scallion. Cut off the root tip and top 2 inches of the green end and discard them. Cut the remaining white and green parts into ¼-inch pieces and put them in a medium-size bowl.

Wash the celery, trim and discard the ends and cut the stalk into ¼-inch slices. Add them to the bowl.

When the eggs have finished cooking, drain them, then cover them with cold water. To speed the cooling process, change the water again after another minute. When the eggs are cool to the touch, roll them around on the counter, pressing down so the shells develop many cracks. The shells should peel off easily. You can run them under cold water to get the last bits off.

Cut the peeled eggs into eighths. Cut those pieces into quarters and add them to the bowl. Add the mayonnaise, sour cream, dill, mustard, salt and black pepper and mix thoroughly. Serve immediately, or chill until needed.

Mom Tip 1
▼

To vary the flavor, substitute ¼ teaspoon curry powder for the dill.

Mom Tip 2
▼

If an egg cracks during the cooking process, or even when you put it in the pan, don't despair. It will cook fine, although it may look a little odd. You will be chopping it up for egg salad, so its appearance doesn't matter. If you're making Mom's Traditional Deviled Eggs (page 126), however, cook a few extra, just in case.

Mom Warning
▼

Don't overcook the eggs or the yolks will begin to turn green. If this happens, the eggs are still safe to eat—although they look funny. If, when you begin to peel one of the eggs, it looks a bit runny, cook the others in simmering water for 3 minutes more.

Mom's Traditional Deviled Eggs

SERVES: 1-2

Preparation Time: 5 minutes ▼ Cooking Time: 20 minutes ▲ Rating: Very Easy

WHAT MAKES THESE EGGS "DEVILED"? Perhaps that's a question for theologians and their chefs. For me, the big question is how to separate the yolk from the white without causing both to fall apart. Actually, the only solution is to not break the yolks in the first place.

While my yolk-extraction skills have improved, my deviled eggs often look injured. Luckily, they still taste good. And eating them brings back memories of picnics and potluck dinners. When I eat them at home, I let in some ants and bees to complete the atmosphere.

2	large eggs
2	teaspoons sour cream
1	teaspoon mayonnaise
½	teaspoon prepared mustard
	Dash salt
	Dash paprika

To hard-cook the eggs, put them in a medium-size pot, cover with water and bring the water to a boil over high heat. When the water begins to boil, turn down the heat to medium and cook, covered, for 3 minutes. Turn off the heat and let the eggs sit in the hot water for 15 minutes (**see Mom Tip 2 and Mom Warning for Egg Salad with Dill and Mustard, page 125**).

When the eggs have finished cooking, drain them, then cover them with cold water. To speed the cooling process, change the water again after another minute. When the eggs are cool to the touch, roll them around on the counter, pressing down so the shells develop many cracks. The shells should peel off easily.

Cut the peeled hard-cooked eggs in half lengthwise. Carefully remove the yolks (**see Mom Tip 1**) and put them in a bowl. Some will pop out whole. Others you'll have to scrape out. Mash the yolks thoroughly with a fork.

Add the sour cream, mayonnaise, mustard and salt to the yolks and mix well. Return the yolk mixture to the whites. There will be more yolk than you'd expect. Sprinkle with paprika. You can serve them immediately, but they taste equally good chilled.

Mom Tip 1

▼

Here's how to loosen
the cooked yolk from each half
without tearing the white: With the
yolk facing up, gently bend the white
area around the yolk in all directions.
Then position the egg yolk face down
over the bowl and gently press the
white area just behind the yolk.
The yolk should pop out.

Mom Tip 2

▼

To vary the flavor,
add ½ teaspoon sweet relish or
1 tablespoon finely chopped celery,
or substitute ½ teaspoon curry
powder for the mustard.

Potatoes / Rice

For the cooking enthusiast, there are soufflés and strudel. For the non-cooking enthusiast, there are potatoes and rice. That's not to say that potatoes and rice don't taste good. I'll take a plate of French fries over a soufflé any day. But potatoes and rice take so little effort. For example, to bake a potato, you run it under the tap, poke it with a fork a few times, and stick it in the oven. For rice, you basically add water and heat. If strudel were that easy, Julia Child would need a day job.

The fact that potatoes and rice are frequently served on the side presents a problem. Cooking two dishes at once is about as much stress as I like in my life. Not only do you have to worry about one of them burning, but no matter how much you plan, they will always be done at different times.

Luckily, potatoes and rice can wait patiently for the rest of the meal to be done. Or you can do what I do: just double the recipe and eat the dish for dinner.

Recipes

Baked Potato / Sweet Potato

SERVES: 1

Preparation Time: 2 minutes ▼ Cooking Time: 1-1¼ hours ▲ Rating: Very Easy

D IDN'T EINSTEIN THEORIZE that a lot of the universe's excess energy got trapped inside potatoes? He must have been right because one of my earliest potatoes detonated in the oven. It was not fun to clean up. I called my mom, and she told me three foolproof ways (described here) to cook a baked potato. Make baked potatoes when you're using the oven to cook other dishes, such as Roast Chicken (page 220), and set the oven accordingly.

1	large potato (russet, Idaho or other baking potato; see Mom Tip 1)
	Salt
	Black pepper
	Butter
	Sour cream (optional)

Preheat the oven to 400 degrees or 375 degrees.

Scrub the potato to remove any dirt. Then you have three choices:

▲ Prick the potato with a fork, deep enough to break the skin.

▲ Prick the potato and wrap it in aluminum foil.

▲ Stick a metal skewer or cooking nail through the potato (**see Mom Tip 2**).

My personal preference is just pricking the potato and baking it unwrapped because I can always lay my hands on a fork. My one skewer always seems to be in hiding. The foil method makes the potato skin soft, and I like my potato skin crunchy.

Bake the potato directly on an oven rack for 1 hour at 400 degrees or for 1¼ hours at 375 degrees. The potato is done when it can be pierced easily with a fork or feels soft to the touch. Serve with salt, black pepper, butter and/or sour cream.

To bake sweet potatoes, follow the same procedures, but reduce the cooking time by 15 minutes. Sweet potatoes tend to drip juice while they're baking, so set them on a piece of aluminum foil. Or wrap them in aluminum foil. Baked sweet potatoes are so tasty, they don't need butter.

Mom Tip 1

▼

"Potato" sounds like a generic food,
but numerous types are available.
Russet, Idaho and Yukon Golds are popular
baking potatoes. Red and White Rose
potatoes are better boiled.

Mom Tip 2

▼

Cooking nails are extra-long
(4-to-6-inch) metal nails available in
the cooking-gadget section of the grocery store.
Sticking one of these nails or a metal skewer
through the potato spreads the heat through
the potato so it cooks faster.
Don't burn yourself when you remove
the nail before serving. Pull it out
with a pot holder.

Baked Stuffed Potatoes

SERVES: 2

Preparation Time: 10 minutes

Cooking Time: 65-75 minutes ▼ **Rating:** Easy

Ever play "Hot Potato"? That's a game where you can't touch a ball for more than an instant because it's supposed to be hot. Well, when you cook this dish you can play the game for real in your own kitchen. After the potatoes are cooked, you have to scoop out the insides. I advise that you use an oven mitt or even a baseball mitt to make sure you don't instinctively throw the potato through the window because it is *hot*. But all this maneuvering makes baked potatoes a lot less boring.

2	large potatoes (russet, Idaho or other baking potatoes; see Mom Tip 1)
½	cup sour cream
¼	cup shredded Cheddar cheese or 3 slices American cheese
2	teaspoons dried minced onion
½	teaspoon dried minced garlic
½	teaspoon dried oregano
¼	teaspoon celery seeds
	Dash salt
	Dash black pepper
	Dash paprika

Preheat the oven to 400 degrees or 375 degrees.

Scrub the potatoes to remove any dirt. Wrap the potatoes in aluminum foil or stick a metal skewer or cooking nail through the potatoes or prick the potatoes with a fork, deep enough to break the skin (**see Mom Tip 2 for Baked Potato, page 131**). Bake directly on an oven rack for 1 hour at 400 degrees or for 1¼ hours at 375 degrees. The potatoes are done when they can be pierced easily with a fork or feel soft to the touch.

While the potatoes are baking, place the sour cream, cheese, onion, garlic, oregano, celery seeds, salt and black pepper in a medium-size bowl (the heat of the potatoes will melt the cheese).

When the potatoes are cooked, cut them in half lengthwise. Carefully scoop out the insides with a spoon, keeping each half-potato skin in one piece. Mix the insides with the rest of the ingredients in the bowl, mashing to remove most of the lumps.

Place the empty skins on a baking sheet or ovenproof dish and fill each skin with one-quarter of the potato mixture, piling the excess above the rim. Sprinkle a tiny bit of paprika on top of each half and return the potatoes to the oven. Bake for 5 to 7 minutes, or until the potatoes are hot and begin to brown on top. Serve immediately.

Mom Tip 1

▼

You can buy
baking potatoes individually
(at a higher price)
or by the 5- or 10-
pound bag.

Mom Tip 2

▼

If you have some leftover
ham or chicken, cut it into bite-size
pieces and add to the potato
mixture to make a
main dish.

Greek Roast Potatoes

SERVES: 2

Preparation Time: 10 minutes ▼ **Cooking Time:** 70 minutes-1¼ hours ▲ **Rating:** Very Easy

YOU CAN BAKE POTATOES, fry them, boil them, microwave them or roast them, and they always taste good. Greek Roast Potatoes are especially easy to make when you're using the oven for something else. They're crispy on the outside and soft in the middle. They're easy . . . easy . . . easy.

>   2   large potatoes
>   2   tablespoons olive oil
>   2   tablespoons lemon juice
>   ½   teaspoon dried oregano

Preheat the oven to 375 degrees or 325 degrees (**see Mom Tip**).

Peel the potatoes and cut each into 3 relatively uniform pieces. Put them in a medium-size pot and add 2 inches of water. Cover and bring to a boil over high heat. Turn down the heat to medium-low and cook, covered, for 10 minutes, or until they have partly softened. Drain.

Put the olive oil, lemon juice and oregano in an ovenproof dish or baking pan. Put the partly cooked potatoes into the dish and stir them around so they are completely coated with the oil mixture.

Bake, uncovered, for 1 hour at 375 degrees or for 1¼ hours at 325 degrees. Stir about every 15 minutes so the potatoes will brown more evenly. Serve immediately.

Mom Tip

▼

Cook these potatoes at the same time you're making Roast Chicken (page 220) or Greek Roast Leg of Lamb (page 189). The longer they bake, the crispier they will become.

REAL MASHED POTATOES

SERVES: 2

Preparation Time: 15 minutes ▼ **Cooking Time:** 20 minutes ▲ **Rating:** Very Easy

YOU DON'T NEED TO BE A ROCKET SCIENTIST to make mashed potatoes. All you need is a croquet mallet and some boiled potatoes. You should use a fork or a potato masher, however, if you also want to eat the potatoes.

I like mashed potatoes—they're nearly foolproof, they're cheap and they go with almost everything. I always make extra so I can make Mashed Potato Pancakes (page 139) later in the week.

2   large or 4 medium potatoes (see Mom Tips 1 and 2)
¼   cup milk
2   tablespoons butter
   Dash salt
   Dash black pepper

Peel the potatoes and cut them into 2-inch chunks. Put these chunks in a medium-size pot and cover with water. Bring to a boil over high heat. Turn down the heat to medium and cook, covered, for about 20 minutes, or until a sharp knife pushed through the potato meets no resistance. Check the potatoes occasionally and add extra water if there's less than an inch left (**see Mom Warning**).

When the potatoes are cooked, drain them and leave them in the pot, covered, to stay hot.

Heat the milk and butter in a small pot until the butter melts. Remove from the heat and set aside.

Mash the potatoes with a masher or a fork and try to get out most of the lumps—unless you're one of those people who actually likes lumpy potatoes. This step requires muscle. Add the milk-butter mixture slowly while stirring energetically (**see Mom Tip 3**). Add the salt and black pepper and serve.

Mom Tip 1
▼

When buying potatoes,
avoid those with a green tinge,
which means they've been exposed
to too much light and will taste bitter.
Also avoid potatoes that have begun
to sprout white, alien-looking
growths. However, if your
potatoes have already sprouted,
don't throw them away.
Just cut off and discard the sprouts
and cook as usual.
Store your potatoes away
from bright light.

Mom Tip 2
▼

Any potato can be mashed.
My own preference is russet,
which I always have on hand.

Mom Tip 3
▼

Add more milk
if you want fluffier
potatoes.

Mom Warning
▼

Very few smells and tastes
are worse than burned potatoes.
Cleaning the pot is also a challenge.
So keep that water level intact.
If you should burn the potatoes
anyway, you might be able
to salvage something by cutting
the unburned parts away and
completing their cooking in a new
pot. Don't just add water
to the burned potatoes.
If you do, everything
will taste burned.

Skillet French Fries

SERVES: 1

Preparation Time: 5 minutes ▼ Cooking Time: 10 minutes ▲ Rating: Easy

Everybody likes French fries. Now I don't have to go to the fast-food drive-through to get them. They're very easy and have no mystery ingredients. I don't even need to keep them under a heat lamp for half an hour before serving. Skillet French Fries are thicker but not fattier than fast-food fries, and you don't need a deep-fat fryer to make them.

1   large potato
2   tablespoons corn oil
    Salt (optional)

Peel the potato and cut it into ½-inch slices. Cut each slice lengthwise into ½-inch strips. You can buy a special French fry cutter to do the job, but a knife and a steady hand work just as well. Wrap the raw cut potatoes in paper towels or a tea towel to absorb any excess moisture (**see Mom Warning**).

Pour the oil into a large frying pan and begin heating over medium-high heat. After 1 minute, carefully put 1 potato strip in the pan. If it immediately begins to sizzle, add the rest of the potatoes (**see Mom Tip**). If it doesn't sizzle, wait another 30 seconds and try a second strip. If the oil isn't hot enough, the potatoes will stick to the bottom of the pan.

Once all the potatoes are in the pan, fry for 1 minute and turn them over with a spatula. Continue turning them every minute or so until they have become golden brown. If they start to burn, turn the heat down to medium.

Drain the fries on paper towels, sprinkle on some salt and serve.

Mom Tip

▼

The potatoes will brown
more uniformly if they fit
in one layer in the pan.
In that case, the frying should
take no more than 10 minutes.
If you're frying potatoes for two,
use a larger pan. If you don't have
one, place the potatoes in
several layers and turn them
over every minute or so until
all the potatoes have browned.
This may take about 20 minutes.
Or you can fry potatoes in batches
and keep them hot in a 325-
degree oven after draining
them on paper towels.

Mom Warning

▼

Oil can spatter
when you put freshly sliced
potatoes straight into
the frying pan.

MASHED POTATO PANCAKES

SERVES: 2

Preparation Time: 2 minutes ▼ Cooking Time: 6-8 minutes per batch ▲ Rating: Very Easy

THIS IS A GREAT WAY TO DISGUISE leftover mashed potatoes. But don't cover them with maple syrup. They're not that kind of pancake.

    2   cups leftover mashed potatoes (see Mom Tip 1)
    1   large egg
    1-2   tablespoons butter or margarine (see Mom Tip 2)

Combine the potatoes and egg in a large bowl and mix thoroughly.

Melt 1 tablespoon of the butter or margarine in a large frying pan over medium-high heat. For each pancake, drop ¼ cup of the potato mixture into the pan and flatten out with the back of a spatula. If you like, you can shape the mixture into patties. Cook for 3 to 4 minutes per side until brown.

Depending on the size of the pan and the amount of the potato mixture, you may have to cook the pancakes in two batches. A 9-inch frying pan will hold 5 pancakes. Add the remaining 1 tablespoon butter or margarine to the frying pan before cooking the second batch. Serve immediately.

Mom Tip 1

▼

If you have less than 2 cups
potatoes, follow the same directions.
However, you could use a medium
egg instead of a large one.

Mom Tip 2

▼

If you add 1 teaspoon corn oil to
the melted butter, you'll be less apt to
burn the potatoes. Corn oil raises
the burning point of butter.

How to Cook Rice

THERE ARE NUMEROUS KINDS OF RICE—long-grain, short-grain, wild, brown, white, instant. They all cook in water, but the amount of water and the cooking time will vary. Brown rice takes more than twice as long as white, and instant takes barely 5 minutes. Although instant rice sounds perfect for the frazzled cook, it isn't because it has very little flavor. This type of rice has already been cooked, and your job is to just heat it up. Of course, you then have to eat it. In my view, instant rice gives rice a bad name.

For reference, 1 cup uncooked long-grain rice equals 3 cups cooked rice. This amount will feed 3 to 4 people.

After reading the directions on the package, measure out the appropriate amount of water, add it to a medium-size pot, cover and bring to a boil. Add the rice, return the water to a boil, stir, cover and turn the heat to low. Don't stir the rice while it is cooking, and don't lift the lid too often to check on it because too much steam will escape. Cook for the time specified. Rice sometimes boils dry and burns, so I turn the heat off 5 minutes before it's supposed to be done and let the heat in the pan finish the cooking.

If the rice still isn't fully cooked at that point, add 2 tablespoons water and cook for a few more minutes over low heat. If the rice is cooked and water remains in the pot, take off the lid and cook over low heat for a few minutes until the water evaporates. If you made a mistake and added too much water, drain off the water and then heat the rice for 1 to 2 minutes over low heat to dry it slightly. Fluff the rice with a fork before serving.

PARSLEY RICE

SERVES: 3-4

Preparation Time: 15 minutes ▼ Cooking Time: 35 minutes-1 hour ▲ Rating: Easy

Not surprisingly, Parsley Rice is green. Not only does it taste good, but it's also perfect for St. Patrick's Day. Parsley Rice is an easy way to spice up boring old rice. I like it because it sticks together—thanks to the egg—and thus is easy to eat. It also absorbs sauces well, making it a good partner for Plum-Basted Pork Roast (page 191) and Sauerbraten (page 184).

½	teaspoon corn oil
1	large egg
1	cup milk
1	small onion
1	garlic clove
½	cup fresh parsley (see Mom Tip 1) or 1 tablespoon dried parsley
¼	teaspoon curry powder
	Dash salt
	Dash black pepper
2	cups cooked rice (see Mom Tip 2)

Preheat the oven to 350 degrees, 325 degrees or 400 degrees, depending on whether you are cooking something else in the oven at the same time.

Grease a 1-quart ovenproof dish with the oil. Break the egg into the same dish and beat well. Add the milk, mix and set aside.

Peel and finely chop the onion and garlic. If using fresh parsley, wash it and dry it between paper towels. Cut off and discard the stems and cut the leafy parts into ¼-inch pieces.

Add the onion, garlic, parsley, curry powder, salt, black pepper and rice to the egg mixture and thoroughly combine. Cover the dish with an ovenproof lid or a piece of aluminum foil tucked around the top edge and bake for 45 minutes at 350 degrees, for 1 hour at 325 degrees or for 35 minutes at 400 degrees. Serve immediately.

Mom Tip 1

Fresh parsley is available all year-round in the vegetable department. Avoid bunches that are limp or beginning to turn brown. Fresh parsley keeps for at least a week when stored in a plastic bag in the refrigerator.

Mom Tip 2

To get 2 cups cooked rice, you will need ⅔ cup uncooked rice. Parsley Rice is a good way to use leftover rice, but I like this dish so much that I cook rice especially for it.

CHINESE FRIED RICE

SERVES: 2-3 AS A SIDE DISH

Preparation Time: 5 minutes ▼ Cooking Time: 12 minutes ▲ Rating: Easy

THIS RICE DISH comes with virtually every order of Chinese take-out. I was surprised to find out you could make it yourself without any exotic ingredients—unless you think soy sauce is exotic. It's the soy sauce that makes the rice brown.

Now, whenever I make plain rice as a side dish in another meal, I cook an extra couple of cups so I can make Chinese Fried Rice the next day. Now that I've figured out how Chinese restaurants make their rice, my next quest is to learn how they put the fortune inside the cookie.

1	large egg
1	tablespoon water
1	tablespoon butter or margarine
1	medium onion
1	tablespoon corn or peanut oil, plus more as needed
2	cups cold cooked rice (see Mom Warning)
2	tablespoons soy sauce
	Dash black pepper
	Sesame oil (optional; see Mom Tip 1 for "Exploding Noodle" Chicken Salad, page 76)

Beat the egg with the water. Melt the butter or margarine in a large frying pan over medium-high heat. Add the egg and cook it, without stirring, for about 1 minute, or until firm. You don't need to turn it over. It will look like a flat pancake. Remove it from the pan, cut it into shreds and set aside.

▼

Peel the onion and cut it into small pieces. Heat the oil in the same frying pan over medium heat. Add the onion and cook for about 5 minutes, stirring occasionally, until the onion begins to soften.

Add the rice, soy sauce and black pepper and stir continuously for about 5 minutes, or until the rice is hot. If the rice starts to stick to the bottom of the pan, add a little more oil (up to 1 tablespoon). Add the egg shreds and stir until they're distributed throughout the mixture. For extra flavor, sprinkle with a few drops of sesame oil. Serve hot or at room temperature.

Mom Tip

▼

To make this dish more colorful, add ¼ cup frozen peas when you add the rice. You can also add 1 cup leftover chicken, beef, ham or lamb to make the rice a full meal.

Mom Warning

▼

Never make Chinese Fried Rice with rice you've just cooked. It has to be leftover so that it dries out a little. However, if you insist on using just-cooked rice, double the amount of butter or margarine and oil. I find this version stickier, and I don't think it tastes as good.

Vegetables
Side Dishes / Main Dishes

IF YOU SKIP THIS SECTION IN PROTEST against the laws of nutrition, I'll understand. I used to think that I'd never eat a vegetable voluntarily. Of course, I never would have thought I'd be writing a cookbook either, but here I am writing one and recommending to you a few of my favorite vegetables.

Some heroes will eat anything just because it's good for them. My mom even drank wheatgrass juice once. Not me. If it doesn't taste good, it won't go in my mouth. That's the benefit of being an adult. While George Bush made it all the way to the White House before he finally took a stand against broccoli, I've already stood up against artichokes. I could never understand why anyone would want to peel off a leaf and scrape his teeth on it.

For me, the key is that you don't have to eat vegetables right out of the ground, like Bugs Bunny pulling carrots. You can doctor them, put cheese on them or marinate them. I can't eat spinach leaves, but I love Spinach Spheres (page 162). Cauliflower is okay, but if you add cheese it's great. If you're not a natural vegetable eater, don't treat vegetables as a daily sacrifice you must make. There are ways to get your vitamins without wanting to spit the veggies into your napkin.

Recipes

SIDE DISHES

▼

MAIN DISHES

AL DENTE ASPARAGUS

SERVES: 2-4

Preparation Time: 3 minutes ▼ Cooking Time: 5-7 minutes ▲ Rating: Very Easy

WHEN I WAS YOUNG, my mother would make me eat asparagus. I thought it was cruel, but she insisted asparagus was nutritious and delightful. Now that I'm older, I've gotten over my aversion, and I actually enjoy eating this strange-looking vegetable whenever it's in season (spring and summer). But nothing can ever make me eat Brussels sprouts. So there.

    1   pound asparagus (see Mom Warning)
    1   tablespoon butter or margarine (optional)
         Vinaigrette sauce (optional; see Mom Tip 1)

Rinse the asparagus thoroughly, being careful not to break off any of the heads. Trim off and discard any white part on the bottom of each stalk, usually 1 to 2 inches (see Mom Tip 2).

Lay the trimmed asparagus in a frying pan and add water to a depth of ½ inch. Cover the pan and bring the water to a boil over high heat. Turn down the heat to medium and cook for 2 minutes (if the stalks are about ¼ inch in diameter) or 5 to 6 minutes (if the stalks are ½ inch in diameter). The asparagus is ready to eat when a sharp knife enters the stalk with just a little resistance. This is called "al dente."

Immediately drain and serve. You can add butter or margarine (the heat of the asparagus will cause it to melt) or a vinaigrette sauce, but asparagus tastes fine on its own.

Mom Tip 1

▼

Here's a quick vinaigrette
sauce you can make while the
asparagus is cooking: In a small bowl,
combine 2 tablespoons red wine
vinegar, 1 teaspoon prepared mustard,
½ teaspoon sugar, ¼ teaspoon black
pepper and ¼ teaspoon salt.
Beat them together with a fork.
Slowly add ¼ cup olive oil,
beating continually until all
the oil is absorbed. Pour over
the cooked asparagus
and serve.

Mom Tip 2

▼

Another way to trim
asparagus is by snapping the bottom
of the stalk with two hands—
it will break where it starts to get
tender. Asparagus is expensive,
so you want to use as
much of it as you can.

Mom Warning

▼

The key to asparagus
is freshness. If the stalks
are beginning to turn brown or
look shrunken, don't buy them.
They'll taste bitter.

Basic Broccoli

SERVES: 2

Preparation Time: 10 minutes ▼ Cooking Time: 5 minutes ▲ Rating: Very Easy

ALL ACROSS AMERICA, mothers tell their children to "Eat your broccoli." I used to think my mom made me eat it just to prove she was in charge. "Stupid, good-for-nothing broccoli," I'd mumble. But slowly, I've been able to rehabilitate myself. Now I like broccoli, but I won't force you to eat it. You can if you want: no pressure here.

1	stalk broccoli (about ½ pound; see Mom Tip 1)
½	cup water
	Salt
	Black pepper
1	tablespoon butter or margarine (optional)

Rinse the broccoli. Trim and discard any leaves and the bottom 1 inch of the stem. Peel and discard ¼ inch of the tough outer surface of the stem. Slice the remaining stem into ¼-inch discs. Cut the large buds (or florets, as they are called) into 2 to 3 bite-size pieces each. Leave the smaller buds whole.

Put the broccoli pieces in a small pot, add the water and cook, covered, over medium heat for about 5 minutes, or until a sharp knife penetrates a stalk without much resistance. The broccoli will still be bright green. I like broccoli to be slightly crunchy. If it is cooked too long, it will become mushy and dull green.

Drain the broccoli and sprinkle with salt and black pepper. It tastes fine without butter, but if you want the extra flavor, add the butter or margarine now. The heat of the broccoli will melt it. Serve immediately.

Mom Tip 1

▼

When buying broccoli,
look for tight, dark green buds.
Some broccoli may be sold as
"broccoli crowns," which
means most of the stem
has already been cut off.
The price is somewhat
higher, but if you don't like
fiddling with the stem, crowns
areworth buying.

Mom Tip 2

▼

Leftover broccoli
that has not been topped with
butter can be served cold with
salad dressing or added to
a regular salad.

Corn on the Cob

SERVES: 1

Preparation Time: 5-10 minutes ▲ Cooking Time: 2 minutes

Rating: Very Easy

Buying corn can be an adventure. Since nature designed the husk to cover the corn completely, it is impossible to see whether it's worth purchasing without partly pulling back the husk. Some grocery stores and roadside stands discourage this practice, so you see people standing at the corn display looking guiltily over their shoulder and sneaking a peek at the inside of the corn. What is left, eventually, is a display filled with manhandled corn. But then again, you don't want to be the only customer to buy bad vegetables, so take a look. The kernels should be yellow or white. If they're shriveled, mashed or worm-eaten, nonchalantly place the corn back on display.

> 2   ears corn (see Mom Tips 1 and 2)
> Butter
> Salt
> Black pepper

Cover a large pot of water and begin heating over high heat. You can speed up the process by using hot water to start with. While you're waiting for the water to come to a boil (5 to 10 minutes), prepare the corn.

Remove and discard the husk and take off any remaining silks sticking to the corn kernels. When the water is boiling, add the corn (**see Mom Tip 3 and Mom Warning**). Boil, uncovered, for 2 minutes. Drain and serve immediately with butter, salt and black pepper.

Mom Tip 1

▼

Fresh corn is readily
available in the summer,
although you can occasionally
buy it during other seasons.
Corn kernels can be white,
yellow or a mixture of white
and yellow. Frozen ears
of corn are available
year-round.

Mom Tip 2

▼

Cook fresh corn
the day you buy it, if possible.
The sooner you eat corn
after it's harvested, the
sweeter it is.

Mom Tip 3

▼

If the corn is too long to fit
in the pot, break it in half.

Mom Warning

▼

Don't add salt to the water,
as this toughens the
corn kernels.

GARLICKY TOMATOES

SERVES: 2

Preparation Time: 5 minutes ▼ Cooking Time: 5 minutes ▲ Rating: Very Easy

MY MOM HAS A PREJUDICE against grocery store tomatoes. She's nostalgic for the time when men were men and tomatoes were tomatoes. Now, she says, tomatoes have become tasteless. Thus, she grows her own. Unfortunately, she's not as good a gardener as she is a cook, so most often her tomatoes are the size of grapes. I don't have the heart to tell her that they taste exactly the same as the ones from the store.

This recipe is the perfect way to spice up bland tomatoes. Garlic makes everything better.

2	medium tomatoes (about 2½ inches in diameter)
1	garlic clove
1	teaspoon dried oregano
	Salt
	Black pepper
2	teaspoons olive oil

Preheat the broiler. Make sure the top oven rack is in the highest position, just under the broiling unit.

Rinse and dry the tomatoes. Cut them in half and place them, cut sides up, on a baking sheet or ovenproof pan (see Mom Tip 1).

Peel and finely chop the garlic. Divide it into 4 portions and spread a portion on each tomato half. Sprinkle each tomato half with ¼ teaspoon of the oregano, salt and black pepper (see Mom Tip 2). Pour ½ teaspoon of the olive oil on top of each tomato half.

Broil the tomatoes for about 5 minutes, or until the olive oil bubbles and the tomatoes begin to soften. (Watch them carefully so they don't burn.) Serve immediately, although they are also good cold.

Mom Tip 1

▼

If the tomato halves wobble,
cut a thin slice off the bottom of
each so it will sit flat on the
baking sheet.

Mom Tip 2

▼

Vary the topping by adding
½ teaspoon dry or fresh bread
crumbs and/or ½ teaspoon grated
Parmesan cheese to each tomato
half before adding the
olive oil.

ATHENIAN GREEN BEANS

SERVES: 2

Preparation Time: 15 minutes ▼ Cooking Time: 50 minutes ▲ Rating: Easy

GREEN BEANS BY THEMSELVES would be boring, so I add tomato paste to keep myself interested. It takes awhile for the tomato flavor to sink in, but it's worth the wait.

When I first tried this dish, I didn't cut the ends off the beans, nor did I remove the strings along the edges. At dinner, I wondered why I was chewing dental floss. On the other hand, my dentist does say I need to floss more.

½	pound fresh green beans (see Mom Tips 1 and 2)
1	medium onion
1	garlic clove
1	tablespoon olive oil
1	6-ounce can tomato paste + 1 can water
	Dash salt
	Dash black pepper

Wash the beans. Snap ¼ inch off each end of every bean and pull. If a string comes off, throw it away with the ends. Set aside.

Peel the onion and cut it into ¼-inch slices. Peel and finely chop the garlic.

Heat the olive oil in a medium-size pot over medium-high heat. Add the onion and garlic and cook for 1 minute, stirring frequently, being careful not to burn the garlic. Add the tomato paste and water and stir until smooth and well combined. Add the salt, black pepper and beans and stir again.

Turn down the heat to very low and cook, covered, for about 45 minutes, so that the beans get so soft that they almost melt in your mouth. Stir occasionally to make sure the beans don't burn. Add up to ½ cup more water if the mixture gets too thick. Serve immediately.

Mom Tip 1

▼

The thinner the beans,
the less chance they will have
strings on them.

Mom Tip 2

▼

In a pinch, you can use
frozen green beans, but fresh
beans taste much better.

GRILLED MUSHROOMS

SERVES: 2

Preparation Time: 10 minutes ▼ Waiting Time: At least 30 minutes

Cooking Time: 10 minutes ▲ Rating: Very Easy

I NEVER CONSIDERED MUSHROOMS as a stand-alone vegetable. In fact, I never considered them at all. I usually forget to put them into Spaghetti Bolognese (page 101), and when my girlfriend orders mushroom pizza, I insist on my half having pepperoni. But eager to make up for some transgression, I cooked her a plate of these mushrooms and ended up eating half. Next time, I'm doubling the recipe. They can also be served as an appetizer.

½	pound mushrooms
¼	cup olive oil
2	tablespoons lemon juice
¼	teaspoon dried basil
¼	teaspoon black pepper
	Dash salt
2	garlic cloves

Wash the mushrooms. Cut away and discard the bottom ¼ inch of the stems. Set aside.

Combine the olive oil, lemon juice, basil, black pepper and salt in a medium bowl. Stir well.

Peel and finely chop the garlic and add to the bowl. Add the mushrooms and mix with a spoon so that they are coated with the oil-lemon juice marinade. Set aside at room temperature for at least 30 minutes to let the marinade soak into the mushrooms. Stir occasionally.

Preheat the broiler (**see Mom Tip**). Make sure the top oven rack is in the highest position, just under the broiling unit.

While the broiler is preheating, transfer the marinated mushrooms and any juice into a broiling pan or baking sheet. Make sure the mushrooms are in one layer.

Place under the broiler and broil for 4 minutes. (Watch carefully so they don't burn.) Remove the pan and turn over the mushrooms. Then broil for another 4 minutes, watching carefully, until the mushrooms begin to brown. Serve immediately, spooning the mushroom juices over the mushrooms, if you like.

Mom Tip

▼

Broiled mushrooms can become baked mushrooms if you
are using the oven for another purpose. Follow the same directions
as above, but bake for 15 to 20 minutes at 350, 375 or 400 degrees.
The mushrooms are done when they have
softened slightly.

Cauliflower with Cheese

SERVES: 3-4

Preparation Time: 15 minutes ▼ Cooking Time: 25-30 minutes ▲ Rating: Not So Easy

Cauliflower isn't going to win any popularity contests, but sometimes you have to take a stand in life. I like cauliflower.

Cutting it, however, was actually the 13th labor of Hercules. He failed at it, which is why history remembers only the first 12. But he didn't have his mom around to teach him some shortcuts. The first time I cut up a cauliflower, it took me about 45 minutes. I cut perfect tiny pieces, and it was tremendously frustrating. When I complained to my mom, she explained the cut-and-snap technique detailed here.

2	tablespoons butter or margarine
2	tablespoons flour
1½	teaspoons prepared mustard
	Dash salt
	Dash black pepper
1	cup milk
½	cup shredded Cheddar cheese
½	teaspoon corn oil
1	medium head cauliflower (see Mom Tip 1)
1	cup water
¼	cup dry bread crumbs
¼	cup grated Parmesan cheese

Melt the butter or margarine in a small pot over medium-high heat. Add the flour, mustard, salt and pepper and stir until dissolved. Add the milk and cook, stirring continually, for about 3 minutes, or until the mixture thickens (**see Mom Warning**). Turn the heat to low, add the Cheddar cheese and stir until the cheese melts. Immediately remove from the heat and set aside.

Preheat the oven to 400 degrees. Grease a 1- or 2-quart ovenproof dish with the oil and set aside.

To remove the leaves from the cauliflower, cut across the base, being careful not to cut into the white buds. Cut out and discard most of the core. Snap the remaining cauliflower into 5 or 6 sections. Cut these sections into bite-size pieces.

Put the cauliflower in a medium-size pot, add the water and cook, covered, over medium heat for 8 to 10 minutes, or until a sharp knife penetrates a stalk without much resistance.

Drain the cauliflower and put it into the greased ovenproof dish. Pour the cheese sauce over the top. Sprinkle with the bread crumbs and Parmesan cheese. Bake for 10 to 15 minutes, or until the bread crumbs are brown. Serve immediately. The leftovers are good cold.

Mom Tip 1
▼

Choose a cauliflower that has tight, creamy white buds. Avoid those with brown or black discolorations. But if necessary, you can easily cut those bits away.

Mom Tip 2
▼

Use this cheese sauce to liven up broccoli or leftover potatoes.

Mom Warning
▼

When making the cheese sauce, don't let the mixture boil after you add the milk. If you do, the milk may separate, making the sauce look unappetizing.

Spinach Spheres

SERVES: 3-4

Preparation Time: 15 minutes

Cooking Time: 25 minutes (*including cooking the spinach*) ▼ Rating: Easy

I KNOW THAT SPINACH isn't everyone's favorite vegetable. All the Popeye cartoons in the world couldn't convince me to eat a big plate of it. Yet with a little tinkering and molding, spinach turns into a dish I'll take seconds of. Go figure. Maybe it's because I love stuffing, which is a key ingredient.

1	10-ounce package frozen spinach (leaf or chopped)
3	scallions
1	garlic clove
¼	cup butter or margarine
1	cup dry bread crumbs or prepared crumb-style stuffing mix
2	large eggs
¼	cup grated Parmesan cheese
¼	teaspoon cayenne pepper
¼	teaspoon dried thyme
	Dash salt
	Dash black pepper
2	medium tomatoes (optional)
½	teaspoon corn oil

Cook the spinach according to the package directions (about 6 minutes), drain it and put it in a large mixing bowl.

Preheat the oven to 350 degrees.

Wash the scallions. Cut off the root tips and top 2 inches of the green ends and discard them. Cut the remaining white and green parts into ¼-inch pieces. Peel and finely chop the garlic. Add both to the bowl containing the spinach.

Melt the butter or margarine in a small saucepan and add it to the bowl. Add the bread crumbs or stuffing mix, eggs, Parmesan cheese, cayenne pepper, thyme, salt and black pepper. Mix thoroughly.

Wash the tomatoes, if using, and slice each crosswise into 4 thick slices. They should look like little coasters. Lightly grease a baking sheet or large baking dish with the oil and place the 8 tomato slices on the sheet (see **Mom Warning**).

Divide the spinach mixture into 8 equal portions and shape each into a 2-inch ball (see **Mom Tip 1**). Don't hesitate to stick your hands in there and squish the mixture around. Pretend you're making snowballs (see **Mom Tip 2**). Put each ball in the center of a tomato slice. Bake for 20 minutes, or until the balls no longer look wet and are beginning to brown slightly. Serve immediately.

Mom Tip 1
▼

You can also use
an ice cream scoop to shape
the Spinach Spheres.

Mom Tip 2
▼

You can make Spinach
Spheres ahead to this point and freeze
them (not the tomato slices) 1 inch
apart on a cookie sheet.
When frozen, transfer them
to a plastic bag. Bake them,
straight from the freezer, as needed.
Add an extra 5 minutes
to the baking time.

Mom Warning
▼

You can bake the spheres
without using the tomato slices as
a base, but to prevent sticking, use
a well-greased or nonstick
baking sheet.

Roasted Vegetable Platter

SERVES: 3-4

Preparation Time: 15 minutes ▼ Cooking Time: 20 minutes ▲ Rating: Easy

WHAT COULD BE EASIER than putting some vegetables in a pan, sprinkling on some olive oil and baking for 20 minutes? Eating them raw, I guess. But when I need a lot of cooked vegetables quick, I prepare them this way. Roasting allows them to keep their shape instead of turning into a vegetable mush. They're even good cold the next day.

1	large onion
½	pound medium or large mushrooms
2	large zucchini
2	large celery stalks
1	green bell pepper
1	red bell pepper
2	garlic cloves
	Dash salt
	Dash black pepper
2	tablespoons olive oil

Preheat the oven to 400 degrees.

Peel the onion and chop it into 1-inch pieces. Wash the mushrooms and cut away and discard the bottom ¼ inch of the stems. Cut very large mushrooms in half. Leave the rest whole.

164

▼

Wash the zucchini and celery, trim and discard the ends and cut the stalks into ½-inch slices. Wash the bell peppers, cut them in half, remove and discard the stems and seeds and cut into 1-inch pieces. Peel and finely chop the garlic.

Put all the vegetables and garlic in a roasting pan or ovenproof dish large enough so the vegetables can be spread out in just one layer. Sprinkle with salt, black pepper and oil. Stir the mixture, trying to cover as many pieces as possible with the oil. Bake, uncovered, for 20 minutes, stirring several times during the baking process. The vegetables will soften but hold their shape, and some may begin to brown. If you're unsure whether they're done, try a piece of onion or bell pepper. Don't overcook or the vegetables will be mushy. Serve immediately. The vegetables are also good at room temperature or chilled.

Mom Tip

▼

The key vegetables in this dish are the onions,
mushrooms, bell peppers and garlic. You can add or substitute
eggplant, carrots, broccoli and yellow squash.

VEGETABLE STIR-FRY

SERVES: 2 AS A MAIN COURSE WITH RICE, 4 AS A VEGETABLE

Preparation Time: 15-30 minutes (*depending on how many vegetables you cut up*)

Cooking Time: 10 minutes ▼ Rating: Not So Easy

S TIR-FRYING IN A WOK is probably the easiest way to cook. Almost anything can be stirred and fried quickly. What takes time is cleaning and chopping the raw materials.

When stir-frying a lot of vegetables at once, you may feel like you need a snow shovel to flip everything over in the wok. A spatula and a strong wrist will normally suffice.

Choose 4 or 5 from among the following:

1	medium onion
1	red or green bell pepper
1	broccoli stalk
1	medium carrot
1	celery stalk
¼	head red or green cabbage
¼	pound snow peas
5	medium mushrooms
1	cup bean sprouts
1	small zucchini
6	ears baby corn (available in cans)
½	8-ounce can bamboo shoots, drained

1 ½-inch piece fresh ginger (see Mom Tip 2)

2 tablespoons peanut oil or corn oil

1 tablespoon soy sauce

1 teaspoon sesame oil (see Mom Tip 1 for
  "Exploding Noodle" Chicken Salad, page 76)

  Dash salt

  Dash black pepper

Prepare the vegetables for stir-frying by washing and trimming them. Remove and discard all stems and seeds. Pull the strings off the sides of the snow peas by snapping the top ¼ inch from each end and pulling firmly along each edge.

Cut the vegetables into ¼-inch-thick slices, although you can leave the snow peas, bean sprouts, baby corn and bamboo shoots whole. Put the cut vegetables in three bowls according to the length of time they need to cook:

Most cooking: onion, bell pepper, broccoli, carrot

Less cooking: celery, cabbage, mushrooms, zucchini

Least cooking: snow peas, bean sprouts, baby corn, bamboo shoots

Peel and finely chop the ginger.

Heat the oil in a large wok or frying pan over high heat. When the oil is hot, add the ginger and stir-fry for 10 seconds, or until it sizzles.

Add the onion, bell pepper, broccoli and carrot. Stir-fry for about 2 minutes. The vegetables will not look cooked.

Add the celery, cabbage, mushrooms and zucchini. Stir-fry for 2 minutes.

Add the snow peas, bean sprouts, baby corn and bamboo shoots. Stir-fry for 1 minute. By now, all the vegetables will have softened slightly (**see Mom Warning**).

Add the soy sauce, sesame oil, salt and black pepper (**see Mom Tip 3**). Stir-fry for 1 minute and serve.

Mom Tip 1

▼

Here are three ways to vary
the flavor of this stir-fry:

▼ *Sweet-and-Sour: Add 2 tablespoons
sugar and 2 tablespoons any vinegar
when you add the soy sauce.*

▼ *Spicy: Add 1 tablespoon black bean
sauce when you add the soy sauce.*

▼ *Hot: Add ⅛ teaspoon red pepper flakes
to the oil along with the ginger at the
beginning of cooking.*

Mom Tip 2

▼

Fresh ginger is no more
difficult to deal with than a garlic
clove, even though it looks like it
came from outer space. It's that
brown, knobby, multi-armed
growth lying in a bin in
the vegetable department.
You don't have to take the whole
thing. Break off a 2-inch finger
and buy that. Back home, cut off
a ½-inch piece, peel it and chop it
as fine as possible. Store leftover
ginger in a plastic bag or small
glass jar in the refrigerator.

Mom Tip 3

▼

To make this a more
substantial meal, add slices of
tofu when you add the soy sauce.
Or, after you've completed cooking
the vegetables and emptied the wok,
stir-fry thin strips of chicken,
pork or beef in 1 tablespoon oil
for 2 minutes over high heat.
Add the cooked meat to the
vegetables or serve on
the side.

Mom Warning

▼

Don't overcook the vegetables.
They should be crunchy,
not mushy.

Vegetarian Chili

SERVES: 6-8

Preparation Time: 20 minutes ▼ Cooking Time: 25-30 minutes ▲ Rating: Not So Easy

When I first heard of Vegetarian Chili, I was skeptical. It sounded as plausible as Meatless Meat Loaf or Diet Fudge. But chili doesn't have to be what it was to the cowboys around the campfire in the Wild West. This recipe is more like a big pot of cooked vegetables. But it does have the requisite beans.

I used to feel that a meal wasn't done until I'd eaten meat. But a plate of Vegetarian Chili is just as filling as chili with meat (**see Chili con Carne, page 178**). This recipe takes major time, however, so I make a lot at once and freeze portions.

1	large onion
2	garlic cloves
3	large celery stalks
3	large carrots
1	small head cauliflower
2	tablespoons corn oil
1	teaspoon chili powder
1	teaspoon dried oregano
1	teaspoon dried basil
1	teaspoon ground cumin
½	teaspoon salt
½	teaspoon black pepper
1	15-ounce can ready-cut tomatoes (see Mom Tip 2 for Bacon and Tomato Soup, page 41)

1   8-ounce can tomato sauce

½   cup uncooked rice

1   cup water

1   28-ounce can red kidney beans

Peel the onion and chop it into 1-inch pieces. Peel and finely chop the garlic. Wash the celery stalks, trim and discard the ends and cut the stalks into ½-inch slices. Set aside.

Peel the carrots, trim and discard the ends and cut the rest into ¼-inch slices. Set aside.

Remove and discard the cauliflower leaves by cutting across the base of the cauliflower, being careful not to cut into the white buds. Cut out and discard most of the core. Break the remaining cauliflower into 5 or 6 sections. Cut the large ones into 2 or 3 bite-size pieces and leave the small ones whole. Set aside.

Heat the oil in a large pot over medium heat. Add the onion, garlic and celery and cook for 1 minute, stirring frequently. Stir in the chili powder, oregano, basil, cumin, salt and black pepper.

Add the carrots, cauliflower, tomatoes and their liquid, tomato sauce, rice and water. Drain the kidney beans, discarding their liquid. Add the beans to the pot and mix thoroughly.

When the mixture begins to bubble, turn down the heat to low, cover the pot, and cook, stirring every 10 minutes or so, for 20 to 25 minutes, or until the rice is soft. Taste before serving. It will look like a vegetable stew. Serve immediately.

Mom Tip 1

▼

Vegetables you can add
or substitute include green beans,
potatoes, zucchini or green or red bell
peppers. Add them when you
add the carrots.

Mom Tip 2

▼

Serve leftover Vegetarian Chili
as a soup by adding extra water.
If the soup tastes too bland,
add ¼ teaspoon of each of the
following spices: chili powder,
dried oregano, dried basil,
ground cumin.

Beef / Lamb / Pork

Benjamin Franklin said, "Man must eat to live, not live to eat." I guess that's why he didn't write *Poor Richard's Cookbook*. I, on the other hand, enjoy a good meal. Judging by Benjy's picture on the hundred-dollar bill, so did he. No doubt he ate his share of mutton. But he probably didn't know about stir-fry or Sweet-and-Sour Pork Chops.

I didn't either, at first. I realized I had a lot to learn when I looked at the thick red slabs of raw meat at the butcher counter. I knew beef didn't grow on trees, but what did a slice of roast beef look like before it got on my plate? This is one time when I really did shout "Help!" The butcher answered.

My girlfriend is a vegetarian, but she's understanding about my craving for meat. She will sit quietly eating a salad while I squat on the floor and gnaw on a carcass.

Recipes

Beef and Cucumber Stir-Fry

SERVES: 2-3

Preparation Time: 20 minutes ▼ Cooking Time: 10 minutes ▲ Rating: Easy

Beef, cucumber and honey? It sounds like an odd combination. But I guess that's how the art of cooking began—taking strange, unrelated plants and animal parts and putting them together over a fire.

I assumed Beef and Cucumber Stir-Fry would be gross. I only tried it because my mom insisted, and I was very happily surprised. The cucumber makes it crunchy, and the honey gives it a slightly sweet taste. Serve this with rice.

¾	pound beef steak (sirloin, rump or top loin; see Mom Warning)
2	tablespoons honey
2	tablespoons soy sauce
¼	teaspoon chili powder
1	cucumber
1	red bell pepper (see Mom Tip 1)
4	scallions
3	garlic cloves
2	tablespoons corn oil or peanut oil

Slice the beef into strips ¼ inch wide and 3 inches long, trimming away all the fat (see Mom Tip 2). Put in a bowl and mix with honey, soy sauce and chili powder. Set aside while preparing the vegetables.

Peel the cucumber and slice lengthwise. Scrape out and discard the seeds. Cut into strips ¼ inch wide and 2 inches long. Wash the red bell pepper and cut it in half. Remove and discard the stem and seeds. Then slice the pepper into strips ¼ inch wide and 2 inches long. Wash the scallions. Cut off the root tips and top 2 inches of the green ends and discard them. Cut the remaining white and green parts into ½-inch pieces. Peel and finely chop the garlic. Set the vegetables aside.

Heat 1 tablespoon of the oil in a wok or frying pan over high heat. Remove the steak strips from the bowl, keeping any remaining liquid (marinade) in the bowl, and add the steak to the wok. Stir-fry for 1 minute; that is, stir continually with a large spoon or spatula so that the contents of the wok cook quickly on all sides. When the meat is no longer pink, return it to the bowl containing the marinade.

Wipe out the wok so that any remaining honey doesn't burn. Heat the remaining 1 tablespoon oil in the wok over high heat and stir-fry the cucumber, red bell pepper, scallions and garlic for about 2 minutes, or until the vegetables just begin to soften. They should stay fairly crisp. Quickly return the steak and any remaining marinade to the wok and heat for 1 minute, or just until the steak gets hot and the liquid boils. Serve immediately.

Mom Tip 1

▼

If you don't like red bell pepper, substitute snow peas. Pull the strings off the sides of the snow peas by snapping the top ¼ inch from each end and pulling firmly along each edge; discard. Add the snow peas when you add the cucumber.

Mom Tip 2

▼

Partly freezing the raw beef makes it easier to slice thin.

Mom Warning

▼

The meat you buy for this dish is important. Get sirloin, porterhouse, rib, rump, New York strip or loin steak, which are tender. Round steak isn't. If you mistakenly buy round steak, slice it paper-thin and cook it for only 10 to 15 seconds, just until it begins to lose its red color. If in doubt about which steak to buy, ask the store butcher.

Beef Stroganoff

SERVES: 2-3

Preparation Time: 15 minutes ▼ Cooking Time: 8 minutes ▲ Rating: Easy

THERE IS A DIZZYING ARRAY of different cuts of steak. I just pick the one with the least fat. In my quest for fatless steak, I once bought "bottom round," which had no fat at all. But each mouthful took five minutes to chew. I later found out that this cut has to cook for a couple of hours to get tender. So now I read the labels as well as scope for cellulite. When I do find fat, I get out my surgical tools to get rid of it.

Beef Stroganoff is an old Russian dish, so how can it have ketchup and mustard as ingredients? My mom informs me that these are her refinements, and they are actually the key to the recipe. She swears she's not thinking of hot dogs. Serve this with rice, plain pasta or Real Mashed Potatoes (page 135).

1	large onion
½	pound medium mushrooms
¾	pound beef steak (sirloin, rump or top loin)
	Dash black pepper
2	tablespoons corn oil
1	tablespoon ketchup
1	teaspoon prepared mustard
½	cup canned condensed beef broth (see Mom Tip)
¼	cup sour cream

Peel and thinly slice the onion. Wash the mushrooms and cut away and discard the bottom ¼ inch of the stems. Cut the mushrooms into quarters and set aside.

Slice the meat into strips ½ inch wide and 1 inch long, trimming away all fat (**see Mom Tip 2 for Beef and Cucumber Stir-Fry, page 175**). Sprinkle with black pepper.

Heat the oil in a frying pan over medium-high heat. Add the onion and mushrooms and cook for 3 minutes, stirring occasionally, until they just begin to soften. Add the beef and cook for about 1 minute if you like meat rare, 3 minutes if you like meat well-done. Stir frequently until the meat has browned on all sides.

Add the ketchup, mustard and beef broth. Bring to a boil and cook for 1 minute. Add the sour cream, stir, heat through and serve immediately.

Mom Tip

▼

Condensed beef broth comes in 10-ounce cans
and is found in the canned soup section. There is no need for salt
in this dish because the beef broth contains plenty.

CHILI CON CARNE

SERVES: 3-4

Preparation Time: 15 minutes ▼ Cooking Time: 65 minutes ▲ Rating: Easy

WHILE EATING CHILE CON CARNE, I sit in my air-conditioned apartment and pretend I'm a gold-rusher warming myself next to a campfire. I exaggerate. However, this is a traditional one-pot meal that can be cooked on the stove as easily as on an open fire. Serve with rice.

1	medium onion
1	garlic clove
1	pound lean ground beef or ground turkey
1	15-ounce can ready-cut tomatoes (see Mom Tip 2 for Bacon and Tomato Soup, page 41)
1	cup water
1	tablespoon chili powder (see Mom Tip 1)
1	teaspoon ground cumin
¼	teaspoon black pepper
	Dash salt
1	15-ounce can pinto or kidney beans

Peel the onion and chop it into small pieces. Peel and finely chop the garlic and set aside.

Cook the beef or turkey in a large dry frying pan over medium heat, stirring occasionally, until the meat browns. This process takes about 10 minutes. After the meat has browned, drain any fat by covering the pan with a lid and carefully pouring the liquid into an empty can. Throw away the can.

Stir in the onion, garlic, tomatoes and their liquid, water, chili powder, cumin, black pepper and salt. Cook, covered, over low heat for 30 minutes, stirring occasionally. The mixture should be bubbling rather than boiling vigorously, and plenty of liquid should remain in the pan throughout the cooking period.

Drain the beans and add them to the chili, stirring thoroughly. Continue cooking, covered, over low heat for another 30 minutes (**see Mom Tip 2**). Ladle into bowls and serve.

Mom Tip 1

▼

How hot should chili be?
It's up to you.
The amount of chili powder
called for in this recipe provides
tingle, not burn. You can make it
spicier by adding more chili powder,
hot pepper sauce or cut-up jalapeño
peppers. Chili powder is actually a
blend of chili peppers, cumin,
oregano and garlic. It comes
in mild and spicy blends.

Mom Tip 2

▼

Chili should be thick
yet slightly runny. Near the end
of cooking, if the mixture seems too
thick, add up to ½ cup more water. If
it seems too runny, take the lid off
and continue cooking to let some
of the liquid evaporate.

Mom Tip 3

▼

Use leftover chili
to fill taco shells or tortillas
or to convert a hot dog into
a chili dog.

Pan-Fried Steak

SERVES: 1

Preparation Time: 5 minutes (*steak*), 2 minutes (*Mustard Sauce*)
Cooking Time: 4-6 minutes ▼ Rating: Very Easy

NOTHING IS OBVIOUS TO A COOK LIKE ME, but apparently the obvious ways to cook a steak are grilling or broiling. Pan-frying works just as well. I found it hard to imagine that a steak would be done after five minutes in a frying pan, but it was. The only challenge to cooking a good steak is differentiating among the many cuts of beef. Serve with Real Mashed Potatoes (page 135).

1	beef steak, about ⅓ pound, boneless, or ¾ pound, with bone (see Mom Tip 1)
¼	teaspoon coarsely ground black pepper
⅛	teaspoon garlic powder

Mustard Sauce (optional)

1	tablespoon butter, softened to room temperature
½	teaspoon prepared mustard
½	teaspoon lemon juice
1	teaspoon butter
1	teaspoon olive oil

Trim away as much fat as possible from the edges of the steak. Pat the steak dry with a paper towel to prevent the oil from spattering when you begin cooking. Place the steak on a plate.

Combine the black pepper and garlic powder in a small dish (**see Mom Warning**). With the back of a spoon, rub half the mixture onto one side of the steak. Turn the steak over and rub the rest of the mixture onto the other side.

Prepare the Mustard Sauce, if using, by mashing the 1 tablespoon butter, mustard and lemon juice together with a fork. Set aside.

Heat the 1 teaspoon butter and olive oil in a frying pan over medium-high heat. When the butter bubbles, put the steak in the pan. For medium-rare, cook a ½-inch-thick steak for 2 minutes per side. For well-done, cook a ½-inch-thick steak for 3 minutes per side. For thicker steaks, add an extra 1 to 2 minutes per side for medium-rare or well-done (**see Mom Tip 2**). Serve with Mustard Sauce.

Mom Tip 1
▼

Numerous cuts of steak can be pan-fried. Look for steaks labeled Delmonico, filet mignon, New York strip, porterhouse, rib, rib eye, rump, shell, sirloin, T-bone or top loin. Do not buy chuck or round steak for this recipe because those cuts require longer cooking.

Mom Tip 2
▼

To check the steak for doneness, cut into it surreptitiously.

Mom Warning
▼

Don't salt the steak until you're ready to eat it. Salt draws meat juices to the surface, and it's better to keep those juices inside the meat when it's in the frying pan.

SHISH KEBAB

SERVES: 2-3

Preparation Time: 15 minutes ▼ Waiting Time: 15 minutes or up to 2 hours

Cooking Time: 4-6 minutes ▲ Rating: Very Easy

I'VE HAD SHISH KEBAB at home since my parents weaned me off of applesauce and crushed peas. Yet now that I see the words "shish kebab" on paper, it seems more like an imaginary food from a children's book than a real meal. Sort of like, "The purple dragon grazed in the meadow, feeding on wild shish kebab." But in actuality, this is a simple-to-prepare meat dish cooked on skewers. Be sure to remove the meat from the skewer before eating unless you're a sword swallower. Serve with rice.

¾   pound beef steak (sirloin, rump or top loin), 1 inch thick

¼   cup olive oil

2   tablespoons red wine vinegar

1   tablespoon prepared mustard

1   teaspoon dried oregano

½   teaspoon celery seeds

½   teaspoon garlic powder

½   teaspoon black pepper

1   bay leaf

½   pound large mushrooms

12   cherry tomatoes (see Mom Tip 1)

Trim and discard all fat from the steak. Cut the meat into 1-inch cubes and transfer them to a large glass bowl or plastic container.

Combine the oil, vinegar, mustard, oregano, celery seeds, garlic powder, black pepper and bay leaf in a small pot and bring to a boil over high heat. Pour this marinade over the steak cubes and mix well. Cover the container and refrigerate for at least 2 hours or overnight. If you are very eager to eat, you can cheat on the marinating time but try to let the meat soak for at least 15 minutes.

Preheat the broiler. Make sure the top oven rack is in the highest position, just under the broiling unit.

Wash the mushrooms and cut away and discard the bottom ¼ inch of the stems. Wash the tomatoes. Stir the vegetables into the marinating beef and let them sit for 1 minute so they get coated with marinade. Remove and discard the bay leaf.

Thread the steak cubes onto metal or bamboo skewers (**see Mom Tip 2**), alternating whole mushrooms and whole tomatoes with the beef. Place the filled skewers on a baking sheet or pan to catch the drippings and broil for 2 to 3 minutes per side. Watch carefully so they don't overcook. Transfer the skewers to plates and serve. Discard the marinade.

Mom Tip 1

▼

In addition to mushrooms
and tomatoes, you can add pieces
of red or green bell pepper, onion or
chunks of zucchini to the skewers.

Mom Tip 2

▼

Ten-inch bamboo skewers
are usually available in the kitchen-
gadget section of the grocery store.
Some cooks advise soaking them in
water for 10 minutes before using
them so that they don't catch fire,
but I've never found that necessary.
Maybe it's because I cram them
with meat and vegetables so
that almost no wood
is showing.

Sauerbraten

SERVES: 6-8

Preparation Time: 20 minutes ▼ Cooking Time: 2½ hours ▲ Rating: Easy

THERE ARE TWO REASONS to cook a large meat dish. One is that you're cooking for a crowd, and the other is that you're cooking just for yourself, but you don't want to cook for the rest of the week. It's really convenient to have leftover meat in the fridge that you can gnaw on whenever you're hungry.

"Sauerbraten" is the German word for "sour roast." Vinegar does indeed make it a little sour, but nothing like a lemon popsicle. Like my other sweet-and-sour favorites, Sauerbraten has a mysteriously spicy taste. Traditionally, this dish would take a few days to make, because the meat is marinated. This recipe uses a shortcut (slicing the meat in the middle of cooking), and it only takes two and a half hours. In relative terms, this is "instant" pot roast. Serve with Parsley Rice (page 142).

¼	cup flour
1	2-3-pound boneless beef roast (cross-rib, chuck or round)
1	tablespoon corn oil
¾	cup water
2	medium onions
½	cup red wine vinegar
¼	cup red wine (optional)
3	tablespoons brown sugar
½	teaspoon black pepper
⅛	teaspoon ground allspice
⅛	teaspoon ground cloves
1	bay leaf

Put the flour on a large plate and roll the meat in the flour until it is completely covered.

Heat the oil in a large pot over medium-high heat. Add the flour-covered meat and brown it quickly on all sides. Add the water, turn down the heat to low and cook, covered, for 1 hour.

While the meat is cooking, peel the onions, cut them into quarters and set aside.

When the meat has cooked for 1 hour, turn off the heat and transfer the meat to a cutting board or plate. Slice it as thin as possible. Add the onions, vinegar, wine (if using), brown sugar, black pepper, allspice, cloves and bay leaf to the pot. Arrange the meat slices in the pot.

Return to a simmer over medium heat and simmer, covered, over very low heat for 1½ hours (**see Mom Warning**). The slices will be very tender when poked with a fork. Before serving, remove and discard the bay leaf. Serve the liquid the meat cooked in as gravy.

Mom Tip

▼

This dish tastes even better
the second day because the spices
have had more of a chance
to soak in.

Mom Warning

▼

Make sure all the liquid
doesn't boil away during cooking.
If the level of liquid at the bottom
of the pot falls below 1 inch,
add ½ cup water.

Roast Beef and Yorkshire Pudding

SERVES: 6-8

Preparation Time: 5 minutes (*Roast Beef*), 5 minutes (*Yorkshire Pudding*)

Cooking Time: 70 minutes-2¼ hours (*Roast Beef*), 30 minutes (*Yorkshire Pudding*)

Waiting Time: 2 hours for beef to reach room temperature before cooking ▼ Rating: Easy

WHEN I COOK ROAST BEEF, which means putting it into the oven and turning on the heat, I sheepishly accept praise for it even though I didn't raise the cow.

Yorkshire Pudding is not a dessert. It is an English side dish made of flour, milk and eggs and is cooked in the roasting pan after you take out the beef. To me, Roast Beef and Yorkshire Pudding go together like peanut butter goes with jelly, but I was born in England, where people eat these things like pizza. Serve with Greek Roast Potatoes (page 134).

Roast Beef

1	3-pound cut of beef suitable for roasting (see Mom Tip 1, page 188)
	Dash black pepper
	Dash garlic powder

Yorkshire Pudding

1	cup flour
½	teaspoon salt
2	large eggs
¾	cup milk
¼	cup water
1-2	tablespoons butter or margarine, if needed

Roast Beef: Remove the roast beef from the refrigerator (**see Mom Tip 2, page 188**) 2 hours before cooking to allow it to reach room temperature. When you are ready to cook it, preheat the oven to 325 degrees. Place the beef, fat side up, on a rack in a roasting pan and sprinkle it with black pepper and garlic powder. If you don't have a rack, just put the beef into the pan. If the roast is boneless, cook it for 25 minutes per pound (rare), 30 minutes per pound (medium) or 35 minutes per pound (well done). Consider using a meat thermometer (**see Mom Tip 3, page 188**). If it's a rib roast, cook it 20 minutes per pound (rare), 25 minutes per pound (medium) or 30 minutes per pound (well-done).

When the roast has finished cooking, remove it from the oven and set it on a platter or carving board and let it rest for at least 15 minutes (or 30 minutes if you're waiting for the Yorkshire Pudding to bake) before slicing.

Yorkshire Pudding: Increase the oven temperature to 400 degrees when you take the roast beef out of the oven. Combine the flour and salt in a large bowl. Add the eggs and milk and stir until well combined. Add the water and beat vigorously.

Traditional Yorkshire Pudding bakes in the beef drippings left in the roasting pan after the cooked roast beef has been removed. Today, however, beef fat may be trimmed back so much that there are virtually no drippings at the end of cooking. You can remedy this situation by adding butter or margarine. Use the following guide:

If the pan has a lot of drippings, remove and discard all but 2 tablespoons. If not, add enough butter or margarine to the pan to bring the amount up to 2 tablespoons.

Return the pan to the oven briefly to heat the drippings/butter. Remove the pan from the oven and pour the batter in. Return the pan to the oven and bake for 20 minutes. Turn down the heat to 350 degrees and bake for another 10 minutes. The pudding should be puffy and brown. Keep an eye on it during the last 10 minutes of baking to make sure that it doesn't burn. Cut it into 8 pieces and serve with slices of roast beef (**see Mom Tip 4, page 188**).

Mom Tip 1

▼

Beef cuts suitable for roasting
include boneless rump roast,
rib roast, rib eye roast,
sirloin tip roast, tenderloin roast
and top sirloin roast.

Mom Tip 2

▼

Many cookbooks say to bring
meat to room temperature before
roasting. I seldom do this because
I usually forget to take the meat
out of the refrigerator in time.
If the meat seems too rare
when I take it out of the oven,
I simply roast it for another
10 to 15 minutes.
Moms aren't perfect.
They're practical!

Mom Tip 3

▼

If you're planning to roast a lot of
meat and poultry, you might want to
buy a meat thermometer. They cost
anywhere from $4 to $10. The
thermometer looks like a clock face
stuck to a metal spike. You push the
spike into the thickest part of the
meat, not touching a bone, and as the
roast bakes, the internal temperature
registers on the clock face.
My butcher suggests an alternative
method: Stick the thermometer into
the meat near the end of cooking,
leave it in place for a minute and
then check the temperature.
For years, I cooked without a meat
thermometer, and I had very few
disasters. I have always found the
cooking times reliable.
However, one thing can
throw the timings off: your oven.
Read the information in
Should I Blindly Trust My Oven?
in Cooking Basics Mom
Had to Teach Me (page 12).

Mom Tip 4

▼

If the roast is underdone
and you need to serve it right away,
slice it and place the slices on a
baking sheet under the broiler for
1 minute to complete cooking.
This changes the taste of the
meat and so is not recommended
unless you're absolutely
desperate.

Greek Roast Leg of Lamb

SERVES: 8-10

Preparation Time: 10 minutes

Waiting Time: 2 hours for lamb to reach room temperature before cooking

Cooking Time: 2-3⅓ hours (*depending on size and desired doneness*) ▼ Rating: Very Easy

I ALWAYS ASSUMED that the more people you had to cook for, the harder it was. But big meat dishes are actually the simplest things in the world to cook. You just put them in the oven. The hardest part of cooking a leg of lamb is carving it.

There's something to be said for the Henry VIII technique of just picking up a slab of meat and gnawing on it. But that only works if you make one leg for each person. However, there is another way. If you can find boneless lamb, or have the butcher remove the bones for you ("butterflying"), then carving becomes simple. Serve with Greek Roast Potatoes (page 134).

1	leg of lamb, 5-6 pounds, butterflied (see Mom Tip 1)
1	garlic clove
1	tablespoon olive oil
1	tablespoon lemon juice
1	teaspoon dried oregano
¼	teaspoon black pepper

Remove the lamb from the refrigerator 2 hours before cooking to allow it to reach room temperature **(see Mom Tip 2 for Roast Beef and Yorkshire Pudding, previous page).** When you are ready to cook the meat, preheat the oven to 325 degrees.

Peel the garlic and cut it into 6 slivers. Cut 6 slits, each ½ inch deep, in different places on top of the lamb and insert the garlic. This sounds weird, but it gives the lamb a garlicky taste. Place the lamb, fat side up, on a rack in a roasting pan. If you don't have a rack, just put the lamb into the pan.

Combine the oil, lemon juice, oregano and black pepper in a bowl and spoon the mixture over the lamb.

Bake the lamb for 25 minutes per pound (rare), 30 minutes per pound (medium) or 35 minutes per pound (well-done). Consider using a meat thermometer (**see Mom Tip 3 for Roast Beef and Yorkshire Pudding, page 188**). When the lamb is done (**see Mom Tip 2**), let it sit for 15 minutes on a serving platter before carving it. This last-minute wait will make it much easier to slice. Slice thin and serve.

Mom Tip 1
▼

The butcher will "butterfly" a leg of lamb if you ask nicely. However, this means that you can't do your meat shopping at midnight. Butchers' hours vary, but they're usually working in the morning. The butterflied leg will most likely be returned to you in a netting, which holds the meat together. Leave the netting on the meat until you're ready to carve it.

Mom Tip 2
▼

The French prefer their lamb rare. I agree with them. But you have to experiment for yourself.

Mom Tip 3
▼

Use leftover lamb in Chinese Fried Rice (page 144). Substitute leftover lamb for chicken in Chicken Fajitas (page 208) or Chicken Tacos (page 210).

Plum-Basted Pork Roast

SERVES: 4-6

Preparation Time: 7 minutes ▼ Waiting Time: 2 hours for pork to reach room temperature before cooking

Cooking Time: 2 hours and 40 minutes ▲ Rating: Easy

WHEN I WAS GROWING UP, I would pound the table for this dish. I would not accept fish sticks as a substitute. When I got old enough to cook for myself, Plum-Basted Pork Roast was one of the first recipes I asked for. It tasted as good as I remembered it. And I didn't have to share it with anyone. Serve with Parsley Rice (page 142).

1	3-4-pound pork loin roast (see Mom Tip 1)
1	cup plum jam
¼	cup red wine vinegar
1	teaspoon dry mustard or 1 tablespoon prepared mustard
¼	teaspoon ground allspice
1½	cups cold water
4	teaspoons flour

Remove the pork from the refrigerator 2 hours before cooking to allow it to reach room temperature (see Mom Tip 2 for Roast Beef and Yorkshire Pudding, page 188). When you are ready to cook the meat, preheat the oven to 325 degrees.

Set the pork loin roast on a rack in a roasting pan and bake for 1½ hours. If you don't have a rack, just put the roast into the pan.

While the pork is baking, combine the plum jam, vinegar, mustard and allspice in a small saucepan. Bring to a boil and cook for 1 to 2 minutes over medium-high heat, stirring continually, until the jam has melted. Remove the saucepan from the heat and set aside.

After the roast has baked for 1½ hours, remove it from the oven. Spoon 2 tablespoons of the plum sauce onto the roast and spread it around. Pour ½ cup of the cold water into the bottom of the roasting pan and return the roast to the oven. Cook for an additional 1 hour and 10 minutes (see **Mom Warning, page 193**).

Lift the roast from the rack, and place on a cutting board or serving platter (see **Mom Tip 3**). Let sit for 5 minutes; this will make it easier to slice.

Meanwhile, make the gravy. In a small jar or bowl, mix together the flour and the remaining 1 cup cold water and stir to dissolve the flour. Add the mixture to the remaining plum sauce and stir. Pour any liquid and meat drippings from the bottom of the roasting pan into the plum sauce.

Heat the plum sauce mixture over medium-high heat, stirring frequently, until it boils and thickens. If it is too thick, add a bit more water. Pour into a gravy dish or bowl. Slice the pork roast thin and serve with the gravy.

Mom Tip 1

▼

A pork loin roast, also known as a rib end, looks like a mini standing rib roast of beef. Boneless loin roasts are also available and can be used here, although the cooking time will need to be extended.

Mom Tip 2

▼

Freeze leftovers in 1-portion servings, each with ¼ cup gravy.

Mom Tip 3

▼

Transferring a hot roast from the pan to a cutting board or platter can be tricky. To loosen the meat from the rack, slide a fork underneath it. Then use two forks, one in each hand, to hold the meat and lift it.

Mom Warning

▼

Don't undercook pork.

When sliced, it should be white or just faintly pink.

Pork loin, which has a bone in it, needs to cook for about 40 minutes per pound.

Boneless pork roasts should cook for about 50 minutes per pound.

If you want to use a smaller piece of meat, calculate the cooking time accordingly

(for instance, a 2-pound bone-in roast would need 80 minutes—50 minutes in the oven initially,

then another 30 minutes after you add the water to the bottom of the pan).

If the pork looks very pink when you begin slicing it, bake it for another 15 minutes.

Or if you're pressed for time, slice the meat thin and cook it in the gravy

on top of the stove for 5 minutes.

Sweet-and-Sour Pork Chops

SERVES: 2

Preparation Time: 10 minutes ▼ Cooking Time: 40 minutes ▲ Rating: Easy

I'VE ALWAYS BEEN CONFUSED about the term "sweet-and-sour." It seems like an oxymoron to me. It might as well be Dry-and-Wet Pork Chops. How can it be both sweet and sour? The answer is easy: vinegar and brown sugar.

When I first cooked this dish, I forgot to add the water. It was such an innocent little mistake, but it caused a disaster. Twenty minutes into the cooking process, my apartment filled with smoke. I rushed to the scene and found that my pork chops had turned black, and the sweet-and-sour sauce had burned into a crust on the pan. My meal was ruined, but I couldn't throw it away because it was stuck to the pan. I had to soak the pan for three days before I could pry the charred remains into the garbage. I'll never forget to add water again. Serve with rice or Real Mashed Potatoes (page 135).

1	small onion
1	medium carrot
1	tablespoon corn oil
2	pork chops (about ½ pound each)
¼	cup water
¼	cup vinegar (any kind)
3	tablespoons dark brown sugar
2	teaspoons soy sauce
¼	teaspoon hot pepper sauce
1	tablespoon cornstarch or 2 tablespoons flour
¼	cup cold water

Peel the onion and chop it into ½-inch pieces. Peel the carrot, trim and discard the ends and cut the rest into ¼-inch slices. Set aside.

Heat the oil in a frying pan over high heat. Add the pork chops and brown quickly on both sides (**see Mom Tip**). Surprisingly, this takes only about 5 seconds per side. Turn down the heat to medium, remove the pork chops and add the onion and carrot. Cook for about 5 minutes, stirring occasionally, until the vegetables have begun to soften.

Add the water, vinegar, brown sugar, soy sauce and hot pepper sauce and stir. Return the pork chops to the pan and spoon some of the sauce over each pork chop. Turn down the heat to medium-low, cover, and cook for 30 minutes (**see Mom Warning**). Halfway through the cooking, turn the pork chops over. There should be at least ½ inch of liquid in the pan. If not, add up to ½ cup water.

Transfer the pork chops to a serving dish. Mix the cornstarch or flour with the ¼ cup cold water and pour it into the frying pan with the vegetables. Bring to a boil over high heat and cook, uncovered, for 1 minute. Serve the vegetables and gravy with the pork chops.

Mom Tip

▼

What's the point
of browning the meat?
Tradition says browning improves t
he flavor. Since it only takes
a few seconds, why
fight tradition?

Mom Warning

▼

While the pork chops are
in the 30-minute-cooking stage,
make sure the sauce in the pan
is bubbling gently, not wildly.
If the heat is too high, the
sauce could boil away and
the chops could burn.

Spicy Chinese Pork

SERVES: 2

Preparation Time: 20 minutes ▼ Cooking Time: 10 minutes ▲ Rating: Not So Easy

THIS IS THE FIRST STIR-FRY DISH I ever attempted, and it taught me some basics about this style of Chinese cooking. I found it's easy to look like one of the Three Stooges when you're stir-frying. I didn't set out everything I needed prior to cooking, so I was fumbling around in various cupboards looking for vinegar and sugar, all the while screaming, "The onions are burning! The onions are burning!" Now I plan ahead.

Unlike the typically American meat-potatoes-vegetable meal, Spicy Chinese Pork is all mixed together and has lots more vegetables than meat. Rice can be prepared separately. Stir-fries cook very quickly, but that's because you cut everything into bite-size pieces first, and that can take 20 minutes or more. Serve with rice.

6	fresh medium mushrooms or 6 dried shiitake mushrooms (see Mom Tip 1, page 198)
½	pound boneless pork (see Mom Tip 2, page 198)
2	tablespoons soy sauce
1	tablespoon cold water
2	teaspoons cornstarch or 4 teaspoons flour
½	teaspoon ground ginger
4	garlic cloves
1	medium onion
1	red bell pepper
2	scallions

2   tablespoons corn oil or peanut oil

¼   teaspoon red pepper flakes (or less; see Mom Warning, page 198)

2   tablespoons vinegar (any kind)

1   teaspoon sugar

½   8-ounce can bamboo shoots, drained

Wash the fresh mushrooms and cut away and discard the bottom ¼ inch of the stems. Slice the mushrooms thin and set aside. If you're using dried shiitake mushrooms, put them in a cup or bowl and cover with water. Let them soak for 20 minutes, or until they are soft. Then slice them as thin as possible and set aside. Discard the tough stems and soaking liquid.

Cut the pork into thin slivers. Combine the soy sauce, water, cornstarch or flour and ginger in a medium-size bowl and stir. Add the pork, stir and let marinate for 10 minutes.

Peel and finely chop the garlic. Peel and thinly slice the onion. Wash the red bell pepper and cut it in half. Remove and discard the stem and seeds. Then slice the pepper into strips ¼ inch wide and 2 inches long and set aside.

Wash the scallions. Cut off the root tips and top 2 inches of the green ends and discard them. Cut the remaining white and green parts into ½-inch pieces. Set aside in a separate dish.

Heat 1 tablespoon of the oil in a large wok or frying pan over high heat. Add the mushrooms, garlic, onion, red bell pepper and red pepper flakes and fry for about 2 minutes, stirring continuously. When the vegetables just begin to soften, transfer them to a plate.

Heat the remaining 1 tablespoon oil in the wok. Lift the pork from the marinade, add it to the wok and stir-fry for 3 minutes over high heat. Add the marinade from the bowl and bring to a boil. The mixture will thicken and have a slightly glossy sheen.

Add the vinegar, sugar, bamboo shoots and scallions and cook, stirring, for 1 minute. Return the rest of the vegetables to the mixture, heat through and serve.

Mom Tip 1

▼

Dried shiitake (shi-TAH-key)
mushrooms, sometimes called
Chinese mushrooms, are sold in
plastic bags in the "Chinese foods"
section of the grocery store
or in Asian specialty shops.
They look like dried-up bits of
leather, but when soaked in water,
they reconstitute. Shiitake
mushrooms are slightly chewy,
so they should be sliced very thin.
The stems never become edible.
Shiitakes have an intense,
mushroomy flavor, and they
add authenticity to this
meal and other Chinese
dishes, such as
Chinese Hot and Sour
Soup (page 44).

Mom Tip 2

▼

If your store doesn't sell
boneless pork in precut strips,
you can buy 2 pork chops and
cut the meat into slivers.

Mom Warning

▼

Be careful with
the red pepper flakes.
They make this dish
very spicy, so add just
a few at first.

BAKED HAM

SERVES: 8

Preparation Time: 2 minutes ▼ Cooking Time: 20-80 minutes, depending on size

Rating: Very Easy

A ONE-INGREDIENT, one-step recipe? What is this? Frozen pizza? The hardest part is figuring out what to do with all the leftovers. Serve the ham with Potato Salad (page 78) or Baked Sweet Potatoes (page 130).

1   boneless chunk fully cooked ham (2-4 pounds)

Preheat the oven to 300 degrees.

Because the ham is already cooked, all you need to do is heat it up. Place the ham on a rack in a roasting pan and bake it for 10 minutes per pound. If you don't have a rack, just put the ham into the pan. Slice and serve.

Mom Tip 1

▼

Cooking a larger cut of ham is only slightly more complicated. If you buy a football-size, 5-to-8-pound fully cooked shank or butt half, complete with rind (brown papery skin), bone and layer of fat, cut off the rind and most of the fat underneath, leaving about ¼ inch of fat to keep the ham from drying out.

Mom Tip 2

▼

Leftovers can be used in Slice-and-Dice Ham and Vegetable Soup (page 56), Crustless Quiche (page 122), Chef's Salad (page 73) or Croque Monsieur (page 84). Add 1 cup cut-up ham to Chinese Fried Rice (page 144).

Mom Warning

▼

Don't do what a friend of mine once did. He recalled that his mother stuck cloves in the family ham before baking it, but he didn't remember that they were spaced about 2 inches apart. So he spent half an hour embedding 200 cloves into the surface of his ham, making it taste cloyingly like candy.

▼

POULTRY

WHY DID THE CHICKEN CROSS THE ROAD? To get to my plate, poor sucker. I'll eat chicken anytime, anywhere. I'll even eat it on airplanes. Chicken is virtually impossible to ruin. If it were possible to make chicken inedible, I would have succeeded. As long as you don't eat it raw or forget it's in the oven and discover it charred the next morning, you should eat well.

Turkey, however, is a test of your moral strength in the kitchen. My mom and grandma can roast a turkey standing on their heads. But at this stage in my cooking career, even though I follow the same directions, I lose five pounds worrying about whether it's going to turn out. Will I have to order a turkey pizza for my hungry friends? Inevitably it comes out fine, but at my house when we bow our heads, it's to give thanks that the bird is edible.

Recipes

Caribbean Jerk Chicken or Tofu

SERVES: 2-3

Preparation Time: 10 minutes ▼ Waiting Time: 15 minutes or up to 2 hours

Cooking Time: 10 minutes ▲ Rating: Easy

THIS RECIPE SURE HAS A FUNNY NAME. I had no idea what it was, and by looking at the ingredients, I still had no idea. There were so many spices that I couldn't guess what it would taste like. However, since I had always wondered what would happen to a dish if I added every spice I owned, I decided to try this recipe.

The list of spices here is by no means random, and the chicken tastes quite extraordinary. No spice dominates. It's flavor by committee. You have to try it to understand. A hot pepper is a traditional ingredient, but the weak-of-mouth, including me, leave it out. Serve with rice or Baked Sweet Potatoes (page 130).

¼	cup vinegar (any kind)
3	tablespoons orange juice
2	tablespoons lemon juice
2	tablespoons olive oil
2	tablespoons soy sauce
1½	teaspoons ground allspice
1½	teaspoons dried thyme
1	teaspoon cayenne pepper
1	teaspoon black pepper
1	teaspoon dried sage
1	teaspoon sugar
½	teaspoon ground nutmeg
½	teaspoon ground cinnamon

1 medium onion
1 garlic clove
1 jalapeño pepper (optional)
3 boneless chicken breast halves (about 1 pound)
   or a 14-ounce package firm tofu

Combine the vinegar, orange juice, lemon juice, olive oil, soy sauce, allspice, thyme, cayenne pepper, black pepper, sage, sugar, nutmeg and cinnamon in a large bowl. Stir well.

Peel and finely chop the onion and garlic and add them to the bowl. If you like very spicy food, remove and discard the stem and seeds of the jalapeño pepper, chop it into ⅛-inch pieces and add it to the bowl. Don't rub your eyes before washing your hands; these peppers burn.

Cut the chicken breasts into strips ½ inch wide and 2 inches long (**see Mom Tip 2 for Chinese Chicken with Peanuts, page 215**). Add the chicken to the bowl. Or if you're using tofu, drain it. Then slice it into pieces 1 x 1 inch x ½ inch and gently put it in the bowl. Stir carefully so that the chicken or tofu pieces are covered with marinade. Cover and refrigerate for at least 15 minutes or up to 2 hours.

Preheat the broiler (**see Mom Tip, page 204**). Make sure the top oven rack is in the highest position, just under the broiling unit. Lift the chicken or tofu pieces from the marinade and place them on a rack in a roasting pan. The rack lets the juices drip into the pan, allowing the chicken or tofu to be grilled rather than half-boiled in the marinade. Put the pan under the broiler, and broil the chicken for 3 to 4 minutes per side, until it is completely white and is just beginning to turn brown. If you are using the tofu, broil for the same amount of time, or until it begins to brown. Serve immediately.

While the chicken or tofu is broiling, boil the leftover marinade in a small pot for 2 to 3 minutes (**see Mom Warning**). Serve the heated marinade as a dipping sauce or as a sauce for rice.

Mom Tip

▼

Instead of broiling
the chicken or tofu, you can
cook it on the top of the stove.
Pour the chicken or tofu and the
marinade into a frying pan and cook,
uncovered, over medium-high heat
for about 5 minutes, or until the
chicken pieces are white and
firm, stirring frequently.
Don't overcook the chicken
or it will be tough.
Test for doneness by cutting
a strip in half and tasting.
**(See Mom Warning for
Chicken with Black Bean Sauce,
page 207.)**

Mom Warning

▼

If you marinated chicken,
be sure to boil any leftover marinade
for 2 to 3 minutes in order to kill any
lurking bacteria left from the chicken.
This isn't necessary if you marinated
tofu. Be sure to wash the cutting
board in soapy hot water to
get rid of any remaining
salmonella germs.

Chicken Cacciatore

SERVES: 2

Preparation Time: 10 minutes ▼ Cooking Time: 1 hour ▲ Rating: Very Easy

MY SISTER SENT ME THIS RECIPE for tomato-flavored chicken. At the time, she was living in an apartment the size of a closet and thus had to master the art of cooking on one burner. I figured if she could do it, so could I. Serve with rice or Real Mashed Potatoes (page 135).

3	chicken legs, with thighs attached
1	garlic clove
2	15-ounce cans ready-cut tomatoes (see Mom Tip 2 for Bacon and Tomato Soup, page 41)
½	teaspoon dried basil
½	teaspoon dried oregano
½	teaspoon dried parsley
	Dash black pepper and salt

Cut any fat off the chicken but leave the meat on the bone. Peel and finely chop the garlic.

Put the chicken in a medium-size pot and add the remaining ingredients. Make sure the sauce covers the chicken. If it doesn't, add a little water. Bring to a boil over high heat. Turn down the heat to low and cook, uncovered, for at least 1 hour. The chicken should be falling off the bone.

Mom Tip

▼

Add some sliced mushrooms or cut-up green bell peppers to make this dish more interesting. Serve with plain spaghetti or Italian bread.

Chicken with Black Bean Sauce

SERVES: 2

Preparation Time: 20 minutes ▼ Cooking Time: 10 minutes ▲ Rating: Easy

WHEN I FIRST STARTED COOKING, my salvation in the kitchen was boneless chicken breasts. Since I'm both lazy and naturally squeamish, it was a relief not to have to wrestle with a whole chicken. Cooking became an act of defrosting and adding a few simple ingredients.

Black bean sauce, however, wasn't a simple-to-find ingredient. I wasn't quite sure what it was, and I wasn't the only one. When I asked an employee at the supermarket, he said, "Black bean sauce? Is that anything like barbecue sauce? Because we have that. . . ." Another shopper guided me to the "Chinese foods" section, where I found a jar of black bean sauce. It looks like jam, tastes a little like soy sauce and gives chicken a distinctive Chinese flavor. Serve with rice.

2	boneless chicken breast halves (about 10 ounces total)
1	tablespoon soy sauce
1	tablespoon vinegar (any kind)
1	teaspoon sugar
1	garlic clove
½	red bell pepper
1	small onion
2	tablespoons corn or peanut oil
2	tablespoons water
1	teaspoon black bean sauce

Cut the chicken breasts into strips ¼ inch wide and 2 inches long (**see Mom Warning below and Mom Tip 2 for Chinese Chicken with Peanuts, page 215**). Put the chicken in a bowl and add the soy sauce, vinegar and sugar. Set aside for 15 minutes.

Peel and finely chop the garlic. Wash the red bell pepper and cut it in half. Remove and discard the stem and seeds. Then slice the pepper into thin strips or ½-inch squares—your choice. Peel and thinly slice the onion.

Heat 1 tablespoon of the oil in a large wok or frying pan over high heat. Add the garlic and stir-fry for 15 seconds, or until the garlic sizzles. Stir-fry means stirring continually with a large spoon or spatula so that the contents of the wok cook quickly on all sides.

Lift the chicken pieces from the bowl, keeping the marinade in the bowl, and add to the wok. Stir-fry for 3 to 4 minutes, or until the chicken turns white all over. Return the chicken to the bowl containing the marinade.

Heat the remaining 1 tablespoon oil in the wok. Add the bell pepper and onion pieces and stir-fry for 1 minute. Add the chicken and marinade, water and black bean sauce and cook for another 2 minutes, or until the liquid boils. The vegetables should be crisp rather than limp.

Mom Tip

▼

If the final dish seems
too watery, here's how to thicken
it slightly: Add 1 teaspoon cornstarch
or 2 teaspoons flour to 2 tablespoons
cold water and stir until no lumps
remain. Add this mixture to the
contents of the pan and heat
until the sauce boils.
Stir thoroughly and serve.

Mom Warning

▼

If chicken pieces are too thick,
they won't cook all the way through
in 3 to 4 minutes. Undercooked
chicken is unsafe at any speed.
Be sure to wash the cutting board
and utensils in hot soapy water
to get rid of any lurking
salmonella germs.

Chicken Fajitas

SERVES: 2

Preparation Time: 35 minutes (*including making Guacamole*)

Waiting Time: 30 minutes ▼ Cooking Time: 10 minutes ▲ Rating: Easy

I FIRST HEARD OF FAJITAS when I worked one summer at a Jack-in-the-Box restaurant. That was the home of the "Fajita Pita." Of course, the customers called it "faggeeta" instead of the proper pronunciation, "faheeta."

Traditional fajitas are tortillas wrapped around beef, lettuce, guacamole, onion and salsa. I don't know the origin of the name, but it might as well mean "that which makes you messy when you eat it." But it's worth a whole package of napkins. Serve with Fresh Fruit Salad (page 80) or a tossed salad.

2	teaspoons Worcestershire sauce
2	teaspoons soy sauce
2	teaspoons vinegar (any kind)
1	teaspoon chili powder
½	teaspoon garlic powder
	Dash cayenne pepper
1	large onion
2	boneless chicken breast halves (about 10 ounces)
½	cup Guacamole (page 28)
½	cup chopped lettuce
4	regular-size flour tortillas (about 7 inches in diameter)
1	tablespoon corn oil
	Salsa

Combine the Worcestershire sauce, soy sauce, vinegar, chili powder, garlic powder and cayenne pepper in a large bowl.

Peel and thinly slice the onion and add to the bowl.

Cut the chicken breasts into strips ¼ inch wide and 2 inches long (**see Mom Tip 2 for Chinese Chicken with Peanuts, page 215**). Add the chicken to the bowl and stir so the strips are covered with the marinade. Let sit for at least 30 minutes in the refrigerator.

Meanwhile, make the Guacamole and put it in a bowl.

Preheat the oven to 350 degrees.

Put the lettuce in a bowl.

Wrap the tortillas in aluminum foil and heat in the oven for 10 minutes (**see Mom Warning**).

Five minutes before the tortillas are ready, cook the chicken and onions. Heat the oil in a frying pan over high heat. Take the chicken strips and onions out of the marinade and put in the pan; discard the marinade. Cook, stirring frequently, for about 5 minutes, or until the strips are white and firm and the onions have begun to soften. Transfer them to a serving dish.

To make a fajita, place a warm tortilla on a plate, spread on 1 tablespoon Guacamole, add some lettuce, chicken and onion and top with the salsa. Roll up the tortilla or fold it in half and eat with your face over your plate to catch drips. Have napkins handy.

Mom Tip 1

▼

For a vegetarian version, cut vegetables—red/green bell peppers, onion, celery, zucchini, eggplant, broccoli—into bite-size pieces and marinate in place of the chicken. Stir-fry for 2 to 3 minutes, or until the vegetables soften, stirring continually.

Mom Warning

▼

Don't heat the tortillas so long that they get crisp. They need to remain soft so they can be folded.

CHICKEN TACOS

SERVES: 2

Preparation Time: 10 minutes ▼ Cooking Time: 5 minutes ▲ Rating: Very Easy

WHOEVER CREATED THE TACO SHELL was a genius. Some person in Mexico invented a curved plate you can eat! When they invent a cup you can drink, I'll change my citizenship.

These "curved plates" are actually fried tortillas. Usually I fill them with chicken, but any leftover meat or even Chili con Carne (page 178) will do. They come in boxes and taste like tortilla chips. Serve with rice.

2	cups leftover cooked chicken (see Mom Tip)
1	scallion
1	cup shredded lettuce
½	cup (2 ounces) shredded Cheddar cheese
	Salsa
4	taco shells

Preheat the oven to 350 degrees.

Cut the chicken into thin strips and set aside. The chicken can be served cold or reheated. To reheat, completely wrap in foil and bake in a 350-degree oven for 5 minutes.

Wash the scallion. Cut off the root tip and top 2 inches of the green end and discard them. Cut the remaining white and green parts into ¼-inch pieces and set aside.

Spread the taco shells out on a baking sheet and heat them in a 350-degree oven for 5 minutes (see Mom Warning).

Fill the shells with chicken, scallions, lettuce, cheese and salsa and serve.

Mom Tip

▼

If you don't have leftover chicken,
you can easily cook 4 chicken breast
halves (boneless or with bone, 1 to 1½
pounds) to get 2 cups of cooked
chicken. Put the chicken breasts
in a medium-size pot and cover
with water. Bring to a boil
over high heat. Turn down the
heat to medium and cook, covered,
for 20 minutes. The chicken should
be firm and white, with no signs
of pink when you cut into it.
If you see any pink juices,
cook the chicken for another
5 minutes and test again.
Transfer the chicken to
a plate, and cut it into
bite-size strips.

Mom Warning

▼

Don't overheat the taco shells.
They come out of the package
very crisp to start with, and if they
dry out too much, they will
crumble when you bite
into them.

Chicken Tikka

SERVES: 2

Preparation Time: 10 minutes ▼ Waiting Time: 15 minutes or up to 2 hours

Cooking Time: 5-6 minutes ▲ Rating: Easy

WHEN I WAS LITTLE, my parents used to drag me to their favorite Indian restaurant. But I couldn't stand the food. My preferred meal at the time was liverwurst, so my mom would conceal a tube of it in her purse and serve it to me on Indian bread when the waiter wasn't looking. I'm still not a fan of most Indian food, but I have grown to like Chicken Tikka, which is much less spicy than other Indian dishes. Since I cook chicken three or four nights a week, it fits right into my rotation. To be authentic, this dish should be cooked in a tandoor, an Indian oven that heats up to 1,000 degrees. But it seems to work nearly as well in a frying pan or wok. Serve with rice.

½	cup plain yogurt (see Mom Warning)
1	garlic clove
1	tablespoon lemon juice
1	teaspoon corn oil
½	teaspoon ground ginger
½	teaspoon ground cumin
¼	teaspoon ground cinnamon
¼	teaspoon black pepper
¼	teaspoon chili powder
⅛	teaspoon ground cloves
	Dash ground nutmeg
2	boneless chicken breast halves (about 10 ounces)

Put the yogurt into a medium-size bowl. Peel and finely chop the garlic and add to the yogurt. Add the lemon juice, oil, ginger, cumin, cinnamon, black pepper, chili powder, cloves and nutmeg. Stir well.

Cut the chicken breasts into strips ¼ inch wide and 2 inches long. (**See Mom Tip 2 for Chinese Chicken with Peanuts, page 215**.) Add the chicken to the yogurt mixture. Stir well to coat the strips, cover and refrigerate for at least 15 minutes or up to 2 hours.

To cook, put the chicken and yogurt mixture into a frying pan or wok and begin heating over high heat. Cook the chicken, stirring frequently, for 5 to 6 minutes, or until most of the liquid has evaporated. The chicken will be firm and white. Serve immediately.

Mom Warning

▼

Don't mistake vanilla yogurt
for plain yogurt.

CHINESE CHICKEN WITH PEANUTS

SERVES: 2

Preparation Time: 20 minutes ▼ Cooking Time: 7 minutes ▲ Rating: Easy

IN CHINESE RESTAURANTS, this dish has the more formidable name of Kung Pao Chicken, which sounds like something from a Batman comic book. One time when I ordered it, it was so spicy that I had to drink all the glasses of water on the table. My friends complained. When I cook it myself, I'm very careful about the red pepper flakes. I add one or two.

This dish also tastes fine without the peanuts, if you think peanuts should be left at the ballpark. That would change the name, though, to Chinese Chicken without Peanuts or Chinese Chicken with Peanuts without Peanuts. Serve with rice.

1	tablespoon soy sauce
1	tablespoon vinegar (any kind)
¼	teaspoon sugar
¼	teaspoon ground ginger
2	boneless chicken breast halves (about 10 ounces)
2	scallions
½	red bell pepper
	Handful snow peas (see Mom Tip 1)
1	tablespoon corn oil or peanut oil
⅛	teaspoon red pepper flakes
¼	cup orange juice
1	tablespoon ketchup
¼	cup salted or unsalted peanuts (not honey-roasted)

Combine the soy sauce, vinegar, sugar and ginger in a medium-size bowl, stir and set aside.

Cut the chicken breasts into strips ¼ inch wide and 2 inches long. Add to the bowl and marinate for 10 minutes.

Wash the scallions. Trim ¼ inch off the white root end and 2 inches off the top of the green stalks and discard them. Cut the remaining white and green parts into ½-inch pieces. Wash the red bell pepper. Remove and discard the stem and seeds. Then slice the pepper into strips ¼ inch wide and 2 inches long. Wash the snow peas and pull the strings off the sides by snapping ¼ inch off each end and pulling firmly along each edge. Discard the ends and strings.

Heat the oil in a large wok or frying pan over high heat. Add the red pepper flakes and cook for a few seconds. Add the chicken, plus the marinade in the bowl, and stir-fry for 3 minutes, or until the chicken has turned white on all sides. Stir-fry means stirring continually with a large spoon or spatula so that the contents of the wok cook quickly on all sides.

Add the scallions, red bell pepper and snow peas and stir-fry for 2 more minutes, or until the vegetables just begin to soften. Stir in the orange juice and ketchup and heat through. I know pouring orange juice into a chicken dish might seem like a leap of faith, but it's worth it. Add the peanuts and stir. Serve hot.

Mom Tip 1

▼

Choose small snow peas—
they're more tender
than large ones.

Mom Tip 2

▼

Partly frozen chicken is easier
to slice. To partly thaw chicken
breasts, transfer them from the freezer
to the refrigerator the morning
you plan to use them.
By dinnertime, they will
be partly thawed.

Italian Chicken Sticks

SERVES: 1-2

Preparation Time: 10 minutes ▼ Waiting Time: 15 minutes or up to 1 hour
Cooking Time: 8-10 minutes ▲ Rating: Easy

CHICKEN STICKS ARE EVERYWHERE. Any diner, cafeteria or fast-food restaurant is bound to have some variation. It's the item I order most often because I figure I'll know what I'm getting. Usually they have no flavor and require a dipping sauce. Our variation, Italian Chicken Sticks, is about as easy to make as it is to eat, and it has plenty of flavor. Serve with Skillet French Fries (page 137) or Baked Potatoes (page 130).

¼   cup tomato juice (or 3 tablespoons ketchup + 1 tablespoon water)

1   teaspoon olive oil

¼   teaspoon dried oregano

¼   teaspoon garlic powder

5   drops hot pepper sauce

2   boneless chicken breast halves (about 10 ounces)

½   cup Italian-style bread crumbs (or 7 tablespoons plain bread crumbs
     + 1 tablespoon grated Parmesan cheese)

Combine the tomato juice (or ketchup and water), oil, oregano, garlic powder and hot pepper sauce in a small bowl.

Cut the chicken breasts into strips ½ inch wide and 2 inches long (**see Mom Tip 2 for Chinese Chicken with Peanuts, page 215, and Mom Warning, opposite page**). Add them to the bowl and mix until the strips are completely coated with the marinade. Refrigerate for at least 15 minutes or up to 1 hour.

Preheat the oven to 475 degrees.

Prepare a baking pan or baking sheet by covering it with a layer of foil (for easy cleanup). Set aside.

Put the bread crumbs (and Parmesan cheese, if using) in another small bowl. With a fork or kitchen tongs, remove 1 chicken strip from the marinade and roll it in bread crumbs. Or you can try shaking the chicken strips in a paper bag containing the bread crumbs. I found this method took even more time because the strips folded over on themselves instead of sticking to the crumbs. I've gone beyond my squeamishness with raw chicken, so I just use my fingers to roll the chicken around in the bread crumbs. I find utensils unwieldy for this job, but maybe you won't. Discard the marinade.

Place the bread-crumb-coated chicken strips on the foil-covered pan. Arrange them so they aren't touching each other. Bake for about 8 minutes. The chicken should be firm, and the bread-crumb coating should be brown and crunchy. Serve immediately.

Mom Warning

▼

To avoid salmonella poisoning,
always wash your cutting board and utensils thoroughly
with soap and hot water after handling raw chicken.

Oven-Fried Chicken

SERVES: 2

Preparation Time: 20 minutes

Cooking Time: 40-45 minutes (*breasts*), 50-55 minutes (*thighs, legs*) ▼ **Rating:** Very Easy

IT WAS ALWAYS EXCITING when my roommates came home with a bucket of fried chicken. Each piece looked uniformly delicious. But somehow the ones I got always wound up being batter, fat and bone. To avoid this letdown, I prefer to cook fried chicken myself. At least then I know that each piece has chicken in it. This is my grandmother's recipe, and it's easier and more healthful because it's cooked in the oven, not in a deep-fat fryer. Serve with Potato Salad (page 78) or Mashed Potato Pancakes (page 139).

2	chicken breast halves or 2 thigh/leg combinations
½	cup corn flake crumbs or dry bread crumbs (see Mom Tip 1)
¼	teaspoon garlic powder
¼	teaspoon dried oregano
⅛	teaspoon paprika
1	teaspoon butter or margarine

Preheat the oven to 375 degrees.

Prepare a baking sheet by covering it with a layer of foil (for easy cleanup). Set aside.

Trim any excess fat from the chicken (**see Mom Warning for Italian Chicken Sticks, page 217**). If you like, you can remove and discard the skin (**see Mom Tip 2**).

Combine the corn flake crumbs or bread crumbs, garlic powder, oregano and paprika in a heavy-duty paper bag. Put 1 chicken piece in the bag, close the bag and shake a few times. Remove the now-coated chicken piece and place it on the baking sheet, bony side down. Coat the other piece the same way.

Dot each chicken piece with ½ teaspoon butter or margarine. Bake chicken breasts for 40 to 45 minutes and thighs/legs for 50 to 55 minutes (**see Mom Warning**). The chicken is done when it gives off clear, not pink, liquid when pierced with a fork. There is no need to turn the chicken. Serve immediately, although it is also good cold.

Mom Tip 1
▼

Corn flake crumbs are available at the store, but you can make your own by grinding corn flakes in a blender or food processor or by crushing them in a paper bag with a rolling pin or heavy can. You need 1½ cups corn flakes to make ½ cup crumbs.

Mom Tip 2
▼

Chicken skin keeps the meat moist during cooking. For those people who don't like chicken skin but like a crunchy coating, remove the skin at the beginning and simply coat the "naked" chicken pieces.

Mom Warning
▼

If you're baking chicken breasts and thighs/legs at the same time, begin cooking the thighs/legs about 10 minutes earlier so they won't be undercooked. Or, if you start them at the same time, remove the breasts as soon as they're done and either serve them first or return them to the oven to reheat a few minutes before serving.

Roast Chicken

A 2½-POUND CHICKEN SERVES 2-3

A 3½-4-POUND CHICKEN SERVES 3-4

Preparation Time: 5 minutes ▼ Cooking Time: 1½-2 hours ▲ Rating: Very Easy

THIS WAS MY FIRST RECIPE. Mom had warned me about the loose items inside the chicken, but somehow I forgot to remove them. When I checked on my experiment after an hour and a half, I got a noseful of burning plastic. After a quick call home, I stuck a fork inside the chicken and pulled out the heart, liver and other unmentionables, plus a lot of red juice. When I called her, Mom said to throw away these giblets and cook the chicken for another 30 minutes, and it worked. Serve with Baked Potatoes (page 130).

1   whole chicken (2½-4 pound), thawed if frozen (see Mom Tip 1)

Preheat the oven to 375 degrees.

To start this dish, I'm afraid you're going to actually have to put your hand inside the chicken and take those giblets out. No amount of shaking will get the job done.

Place the chicken (directly from the refrigerator) on a rack in a roasting pan (**see Mom Tip 2**). If you don't have a rack, just put the chicken in a pan or an ovenproof casserole. Bake for 1½ to 2 hours (**see Mom Warning**). To see if it's done, tip the pan so that some juice runs out of the cavity. If the juice is clear, not red, the chicken is ready to eat. If the juice is red, cook for another 15 minutes and test again. If the leg wiggles easily, it is done. Remove the chicken from the oven, cut it into pieces and serve.

Mom Tip 1

▼

Thaw a chicken in the
refrigerator, a process that takes
about 24 hours. Don't let it thaw
on the counter because bacteria
multiply very rapidly
in chicken.

Mom Tip 2

▼

To add extra flavor,
sprinkle the outside with
¼ teaspoon garlic powder and
¼ teaspoon dried oregano
before baking.

Mom Warning

▼

If the chicken is partly frozen,
cook it for an extra ½ hour to
make sure it's done.

Mom Tip 3

▼

Once you've become
adept at roasting a chicken,
you might want to add some stuffing.
This complicates the recipe
somewhat but shows that you're a
whiz in the kitchen.
For how to stuff a chicken,
follow the directions for
Roast Turkey with Stuffing
(page 224).

Teriyaki Chicken

SERVES: 2

Preparation Time: 10 minutes ▼ Waiting Time: 15 minutes or up to 2 hours

Cooking Time: 6-8 minutes ▲ Rating: Easy

IF THERE IS EVER A TRADE WAR with Japan and they decide to cut off the flow of "teriyaki" to the restaurant in my neighborhood mall, it won't faze me. I recently found out how to make Teriyaki Chicken. I used to think that there must be some spice extracted from the obscure "teriyaki" flower in the Japanese countryside. But it turns out that the secret ingredients are sugar, soy sauce and ginger. If Ramen soup weren't so cheap, my next mission would be to decipher *its* recipe. Serve with Chinese Fried Rice (page 144).

3	tablespoons soy sauce
2	tablespoons dark brown sugar
1	tablespoon corn oil
½	teaspoon ground ginger
½	teaspoon garlic powder
⅛	teaspoon black pepper
2	boneless chicken breast halves (about 10 ounces)

Combine the soy sauce, brown sugar, oil, ginger, garlic powder and black pepper in a medium-size bowl. Set aside.

Cut the chicken into strips ½ inch wide and 2 inches long (**see Mom Tip 2 for Chinese Chicken with Peanuts, page 215, and Mom Warning for Italian Chicken Sticks, page 217**). Add the chicken to the bowl and marinate in the refrigerator for 1 to 2 hours so the flavors penetrate the chicken. If you're in a hurry, you can marinate the chicken for just 15 minutes. It won't be quite so tasty, but it will have more flavor than if you hadn't bothered at all.

Preheat the broiler. Make sure the top oven rack is in the highest position, just under the broiling unit.

If you have metal or bamboo skewers (**see Mom Tip 2 for Shish Kebab, page 183, and Mom Tip 1 below**), thread the chicken strips onto the skewers and lay the skewers on a baking sheet. If you don't have skewers, place the chicken in a single layer on the baking sheet. Discard the marinade. Broil the chicken for 3 to 4 minutes per side, until it is completely white and is just beginning to turn brown. Skewers make the turning-over process go faster. Serve immediately.

Mom Tip 1

▼

You can also thread a few whole mushrooms, strips of red bell pepper or pieces of onion between the chicken strips before broiling.

Mom Tip 2

▼

To make Teriyaki Beef, substitute ½-inch-thick sirloin steak strips for the chicken strips and broil for 2 minutes per side.

Roast Turkey with Stuffing

A 10-POUND TURKEY SERVES 8

Waiting Time: A frozen turkey takes 3 days to thaw

Preparation Time: 45 minutes (*with stuffing*), 10 minutes (*without stuffing*)

Cooking Time: 3¼-4 hours (*10-12 pound stuffed turkey*), 2½-3 hours (*10-12-pound unstuffed turkey*)

Rating: Not So Easy

BEFORE I MADE A TURKEY, it seemed really difficult. After all, hadn't I watched my grandma slaving all day over the turkey every Thanksgiving? With so many seasoned cooks in my family, the thought of making turkey myself never entered my mind. But alas, I couldn't make it home for Thanksgiving. Would I be happy with a frozen turkey dinner? I decided to take the big plunge and invite friends to have Thanksgiving dinner at my house.

After glancing at the length of the recipe, I feared this was going to be the worst Thanksgiving my guests would ever have. I was afraid it was going to taste terrible no matter what I did. But since I couldn't back out, I decided to think of turkey as a big chicken, which I had already cooked successfully. By following my mom's explicit directions, I found that turkey was not so overwhelming after all. The tricky part of Thanksgiving dinner comes when you try to make the turkey, potatoes, gravy, cranberry sauce and vegetables all at the same time. But I'll worry about that next year.

Stuffing

1	large onion
2	large celery stalks
½	cup (1 stick) butter or margarine
¼	teaspoon black pepper
	Dash salt

1½   cups water

1   12-ounce bag or box dry stuffing, cubes or crumbs

Turkey

1   10-12-pound turkey, fresh or thawed (see Mom Tip 1)

1   tablespoon butter or margarine or 1 tablespoon corn oil

Stuffing: Peel the onion and chop it into ½-inch pieces. Wash the celery stalks, trim and discard the ends and cut the stalks into ¼-inch slices. Melt the butter or margarine in a large pot over medium-high heat. Add the onion and celery pieces, black pepper and salt and cook, stirring occasionally, for about 5 minutes, or until the vegetables begin to soften. Turn off the heat and add the water and the dry stuffing. Mix thoroughly. The stuffing should look slightly moist, not mushy. Set aside. You can make the stuffing the night before and refrigerate it, but to prevent food poisoning, do not stuff the turkey until you are ready to put it in the oven.

Turkey: Remove and set aside one oven rack and place the other at the lowest position. Preheat the oven to 450 degrees. A turkey takes up a lot of oven space. Get the roasting pan and rack ready. If you don't have a roasting pan and rack, buy a heavy-duty foil roasting pan that has bumps in the bottom to elevate the turkey. Grocery stores sell them around the holiday season for about $1.

Put the turkey in the sink and remove the loose pieces (these are called giblets) from inside the bird. In turkeys, there's an extra place they might be hiding—the small cavity above the neck—so check here, too. Discard the giblets unless you plan to make Turkey Gravy (page 228). In that case, set the giblets and neck aside in the refrigerator.

Rinse the turkey in cold water inside and out, and remove and discard any large white clumps of fat near the tail. Place the turkey, breast side down, on a rack in the roasting pan.

To stuff the turkey, start with the neck cavity, spooning in about 1 cup of stuffing. Then fold the loose neck skin over the stuffing, completely encasing it. To keep the neck skin in place, you have three options: (1) sew it down with a large needle and heavy cotton thread; (2) use a metal skewer to interweave the neck and back skins; (3) hold the neck skin in place with your left hand and flip the turkey over onto its back with your right hand. The weight of the turkey should keep the neck stuffing in place. I use this third method because it's the easiest, and although it's a little tricky, it works. Or you can skip stuffing this area altogether and concentrate on the main cavity.

Turn the turkey onto its back and spoon the stuffing into the cavity until it seems full. Don't pack it too tightly. Stuffing expands when it cooks, and you don't want to become one of the exploding-turkey victims newspapers write about every year. Extra stuffing can be baked in a separate covered container in the oven during the last 45 minutes that the turkey is roasting.

Once the main cavity is stuffed, close the cavity by sewing it shut or using a turkey-lacing kit (needle-like skewers sold in a package at the grocery store). Alternatively, leave the stuffing exposed. That's what I do. The stuffing gets a little crisp on the outside, but so what.

The final step in preparing the turkey is rubbing some butter, margarine or oil on the skin to help it brown as it roasts. Cut 1 tablespoon butter or margarine into small pieces and dab them onto different parts of the turkey skin. Alternatively, wipe the skin with an empty butter or margarine wrapper or 1 tablespoon oil.

Put the turkey into the oven (breast side up) and immediately turn down the heat to 325 degrees. Bake for about 20 minutes per pound. If you decided not to stuff the turkey, bake for 15 minutes per pound. For a stuffed turkey weighing more than 15 pounds, bake for 15 minutes per pound.

If you are making gravy, start preparing it now (see page 228).

After the turkey has cooked for 1 hour and begins to brown, baste it (**see Mom Tip 2**) and place a large piece of aluminum foil over it like a tent to keep the breast from getting too brown. Baste every ½ hour or so. About 1 hour before the turkey is ready to come out of the oven, remove the foil.

Try to avoid overcooking. Here are four ways to tell if the turkey is done: The leg can be easily wiggled; the thigh is soft when pressed; juices from a skewer prick in the thigh run yellow rather than pink; the meat thermometer registers 175 degrees. If the leg is too easily wiggled, the breast will be grainy and overdone.

When you have decided the turkey is done, remove it from the oven and let it sit for at least 15 minutes. Before carving, transfer the turkey to a large platter or tray.

To carve, begin by removing the stuffing and placing it in a separate serving dish. Cut off a leg and thigh and set it on a serving platter. Separate the leg from the thigh and slice up some of the thigh meat. Leave the leg whole. Cut off a wing and add it to the platter. Begin slicing the breast, placing slices on the platter. Don't slice more than you think you'll need. The remainder will be much easier to slice after dinner or the next day when it's cold.

Before you put the leftover turkey in the refrigerator, remove all the stuffing from the cavity and store it separately in the refrigerator. To freeze, **see Mom Tip 3.**

Mom Tip 1

▼

It takes 3 days to thaw
a turkey in the refrigerator.
That's the safest way to thaw one.
You can speed up the process
by placing the still-wrapped turkey
under cold running water.
Don't let it sit in the sink all
day at room temperature because
that process encourages bacteria
to develop in the turkey.

Mom Tip 2

▼

Basting means pouring the
melted butter and turkey juices over
the turkey every half hour as it cooks.
This turns the turkey skin glossy
brown. It's also supposed
to keep the turkey moist.
There is a special utensil,
a turkey baster, designed
especially for this purpose.
It's a long plastic or glass tube
with a bulbous rubber handle that
you squeeze to suck liquid into
the tube. If you don't have one,
use a large spoon to collect the
juices and spoon them
over the bird.

Mom Tip 3

▼

Leftover cooked turkey
freezes well. Freeze breast slices
in 1- or 2-serving portions.
Freeze a whole leg
and thigh.

TURKEY GRAVY

SERVES: 8

Preparation Time: 15 minutes

Cooking Time: 1 hour (*giblet broth*), 15 minutes (*making the gravy*) ▼ Rating: Not So Easy

	Turkey giblets and neck
	Turkey giblets and neck
1	medium onion
3	large sprigs fresh parsley
	Roasting pan juices
2	tablespoons cornstarch (see Mom Tip)
2	tablespoons cold water
½	cup hot water

When you begin roasting the turkey (see Roast Turkey, page 224), put the giblets and neck in a medium-size pot.

Peel the onion, cut it into quarters and add the pieces to the pot. Wash the parsley and add it to the pot. Cover with water and bring to a boil over high heat. Turn down the heat to medium-low and cook, covered, for 1 hour. Drain and save the giblet broth in a container; discard the giblets, neck and vegetables. Refrigerate the broth.

Measure the cornstarch into a small bowl. Add the cold water, stir well to dissolve and set aside.

When you transfer the cooked turkey to the platter, pour the juices that have collected in the bottom of the pan into a glass jar. The amount of liquid will vary, depending on the size of the turkey and whether you stuffed it. Expect at least ¼ cup of liquid. The grease will separate and rise to the top. A glass container allows you to see the grease. Spoon out and discard as much of the grease as possible. Pour the remaining liquid into a medium-size pot.

Add the hot water to the roasting pan. With a spoon, scrape loose any baked-on bits of turkey stuck to the bottom. Add these scrapings to the pot.

Add 1 cup of the refrigerated giblet broth to the pot and begin heating over high heat. When the broth comes to a boil, gradually stir in some of the cornstarch mixture. When the gravy starts to thicken, don't add any more cornstarch. You may not need all the cornstarch, but it's easier to mix it up beforehand than to stop what you're doing and make more. If the gravy gets too thick, add more giblet broth. Let it boil for several minutes and serve.

Mom Tip

▼

Cornstarch is a thickening agent. It is more effective
than regular flour. One tablespoon cornstarch does
the same job as 2 tablespoons flour.

FISH

THE ONLY FISH I WOULD EAT WHEN I WAS YOUNG came either out of a can or a frozen package. That's because tuna fish and fish sticks had no bones. When my mom would serve fish that actually looked like fish, I would refuse to eat it. While I liked the taste, the fear of having to pick bones out of my mouth was enough to sour me on the experience.

When I started cooking for myself, it took quite a lot of convincing before I would actually buy fish. I used to tell my mom to call me when scientists were able to breed a boneless trout. She told me that in the meantime, I could eat scallops, mussels and squid, which have no bones. I didn't take to that offer.

Her next line of assault was to convince me to buy salmon because the bones were big and easy to remove. That seemed reasonable, so I tried it. It turned out to be surprisingly good, and she wasn't lying about the bones.

After that initial success, she was prepared to ship a boxload of fish recipes. I advised her not to push her luck. Therefore, there are only three recipes in this section, one of which is for shrimp, which I never really considered fish. Apparently my rehabilitation is not yet complete.

Recipes

Fresh Baked Salmon with Garlic Mayonnaise

SERVES: 3-4

Preparation Time: 5 minutes (*salmon*), 5 minutes (*mayonnaise*) ▼ **Cooking Time:** 1 hour ▲ **Rating:** Very Easy

I HAVE TWO MAJOR PROBLEMS WITH FISH. First, I hate having to pull bones out of my mouth. Second, I dislike the lingering smell on my hands. The great thing about salmon is that the bones are large enough to see, and you can take most of them out in one fell swoop before you serve the dish. As for the smell, my mom told me you can get rid of it by rubbing lemon juice on your hands. But how do you remove the smell of lemon juice? I guess you could rub your hands with fish.

Salmon is seasonal and can be expensive. I once tried to buy a whole salmon in a fish market in New York City, and they wanted $40 for it. A few months later in California, I paid $8 for one of the same size. Catching it myself might have been even cheaper, but then I would have had to clean it. Serve this with Parsley Rice (page 142).

½   **fresh whole salmon, about 2 pounds**
      (see Mom Tips 1, 2 and 3, page 234)

Garlic Mayonnaise

¼   **cup mayonnaise**
1   **teaspoon olive oil**
½   **teaspoon dried dill**
1   **very small garlic clove**

Preheat the oven to 325 degrees.

Cut a large enough piece of aluminum foil to fully wrap the salmon. Rinse the fish, put it in the middle of the foil and wrap it tightly so that it can steam in its own juices. Place it on a baking sheet or in a large pan and bake for 1 hour. That's it.

Garlic Mayonnaise: Meanwhile, combine the mayonnaise, olive oil and dill in a small dish. Peel the garlic and push it through a garlic press or mince it. Add ⅛ teaspoon of the garlic to the mayonnaise mixture, stir thoroughly, cover and refrigerate.

When the salmon has finished cooking, remove the pan from the oven and open the foil to let the steam escape. Here comes the tricky part—removing the skin and bones from the fish. While the salmon is still lying in the foil, use a fork to scrape or pull the skin off the top of the fish. Discard the skin.

With a knife, cut the top layer of fish in half along the backbone, but don't cut through the backbone. Insert a spatula or wide-bladed knife into the top layer at the cut and gently lift up one serving of fish, leaving half the backbone exposed. Lift up the second serving, leaving the backbone fully exposed.

With a fork or your fingers, pull away and discard the backbone and its attached bones. To serve the remaining fish, insert the spatula just above the bottom layer of skin and gently dislodge the fish from the skin. Serve with Garlic Mayonnaise.

Mom Tip 1

▼

Fresh salmon is sold
three different ways—whole,
steaks (¾-to-1-inch-thick sections
with a bone in the middle) or fillets
(flat, boneless pieces).
This recipe calls for half
of a whole salmon.
I prefer the tail half because there
seem to be fewer bones, but
that may be my imagination.
If you find salmon that are small
(about 3 pounds), you can cook
the whole fish by the method
described here.

Mom Tip 2

▼

Use any leftovers for
Salmon Quiche (page 236).

Mom Tip 3

▼

Many cooks are puzzled
by cooking fresh salmon, not
realizing how easy it is.
If you fear you'll mess it up,
cook it early in the day so
you'll have plenty of time
to experiment.
Then serve it cold.
For a special occasion,
you could serve this dish
cold as an appetizer.

SCAMPI

SERVES: 2

Preparation Time: 5 minutes ▼ **Cooking Time:** 5 minutes ▲ **Rating:** Very Easy

I ONCE ORDERED SCAMPI at a restaurant, and it took 45 minutes to arrive. I don't know what they were doing to it. Making Scampi at home is really easy and takes only 10 minutes. In case you were wondering, "scampi" is a fancy Italian name for shrimp. It tastes good served with rice.

2	garlic cloves
2	tablespoons butter or margarine
2	tablespoons olive oil
½	teaspoon dried oregano
½	teaspoon dried basil
½	pound cooked peeled shrimp (see Mom Tip 1 for Shrimp Cocktail, page 37)
2	teaspoons lemon juice

Peel and finely chop the garlic. Melt the butter or margarine in a large frying pan over medium-high heat. Add the olive oil, garlic, oregano and basil and cook for 30 seconds, or until the garlic sizzles. Do not let the garlic brown or it will become bitter. Add the shrimp and lemon juice. If the shrimp are already cooked, just heat through. If you are using shrimp that are peeled and cooked but still frozen, cook them a few minutes longer, until they have thawed and are hot. (If you are using unpeeled raw shrimp, **see Mom Tip 2 for Shrimp Cocktail, page 37**). Serve immediately.

SALMON QUICHE

SERVES: 4

Preparation Time: 10 minutes ▼ Cooking Time: 35-45 minutes

Waiting Time: 5-10 minutes ▲ Rating: Easy

IF I HADN'T MISTAKENLY EATEN a slice of Salmon Quiche I found in my mom's refrigerator, I would never have thought I would like it. I had spent the previous semester at college avoiding such delicacies as baked scrod and spinach quiche. Maybe I was wrong not to eat those dishes simply because they didn't sound as good as chocolate mousse. Salmon Quiche turned out to be a staple dinner for me, not only because I like the taste but also because the ready-made pie crusts and canned salmon make this very easy to prepare. Maybe scrod quiche is next. Serve with Mashed Potato Pancakes (page 139).

1   Pillsbury Pie Crust
2   large eggs
1   6-ounce can skinless, boneless salmon (see Mom Tip)
1   cup whipping (not whipped) cream (see Mom Tip for
     Crustless Quiche, page 123)
1   tablespoon grated Parmesan cheese
1   teaspoon dried dill
6   drops hot pepper sauce or ¼ teaspoon cayenne pepper
     Dash black pepper

Preheat the oven to 425 degrees.

These Pillsbury crusts are the next best thing to homemade. They come two to a box and are located in the refrigerated section of the grocery store, next to the tubes of refrigerated biscuits. Follow the directions for "prebaked crust," lining a 9-inch pie pan with the crust and smoothing it into place. Be careful you don't overbake it. Check the crust after it has been in the oven for 6 minutes (**see Mom Warning**). The crust should be lightly browned. Remove from the oven and cool on a rack or stove top. Turn down the oven temperature to 400 degrees.

To make the filling, beat the eggs in a large bowl. Drain the salmon and discard the liquid. Add the salmon, cream, Parmesan cheese, dill, hot pepper sauce or cayenne pepper and black pepper to the bowl. Mix thoroughly, making sure the salmon is broken up into small pieces. Pour the mixture into the pie crust and bake for 30 to 35 minutes, or until the filling is firm and beginning to brown. Remove from the oven and let cool for 5 to 10 minutes before serving.

Mom Tip
▼

You can vary the amount
of salmon. If you can't find the
skinless, boneless variety, use a
15-ounce can of pink or red salmon.
You will have to remove the bones
and skin yourself, however.
Drain the salmon and transfer it
to an empty bowl. Use two forks
to peel away the skin. Carefully
separate the salmon into pieces and
discard as many bones as you can,
especially the round backbones.
Then proceed with the recipe.

Mom Warning
▼

I have burned many crusts
by forgetting to set the oven timer.
To prevent overbaking, check the
crust after it has been in the oven
for 6 minutes and then each
minute thereafter to make sure
it doesn't get too brown.

DESSERTS

MAN CANNOT LIVE BY DESSERT ALONE, but sometimes I think about testing that theory. Pound cake can be a perfectly good substitute for cereal. If I want some fruit, why not blueberry pie? As for the main course, Fudge Pie can almost pass for quiche.

And I haven't even mentioned my all-time favorite food. Some people remember their first word, their first kiss, their first time behind the wheel. I remember the first time I made Chocolate Chip Cookies. I didn't even have to ask my mom for the keys to the food processor.

For years, I was monogamous with Chocolate Chip Cookies. Then I started flirting with Brownies. Before I knew it, I was seeing English Walnut Pie and pound cake on the side. But Chocolate Chip Cookies are still my first love.

Now whenever I visit my sister, I bring my food processor to make her a batch. When she visits me, she brings her vacuum cleaner.

Recipes

How to Bake

W ITH MOST COOKING, you can throw in a little of this and that and not follow the directions exactly but still end up with a good meal. That's not true with baking, which is more like a chemistry experiment. You won't blow up the oven if you add too much baking powder to the brownies, but they might not taste good. You can buy plenty of mediocre desserts. If you're going to the trouble of making your own, take that extra step of accurately measuring the ingredients. Here are some tips:

▼ The Correct Measuring Cups ▲

Exact measurements are important. Buy plastic or metal measuring cups (¼ cup, ⅓ cup, ½ cup, 1 cup), which are crucial for the accurate measuring of dry ingredients, and measuring spoons (¼ teaspoon, ½ teaspoon, 1 teaspoon, 1 tablespoon).

▼ Measuring Flour ▲

When you're measuring flour, don't press it down in the cup (or spoon). Either dip the cup into the flour or spoon the flour into the cup until it is overflowing. Then draw a knife across the top to scrape away the excess flour.

▼ Measuring Brown Sugar ▲

Brown sugar should always be pressed tightly into the measuring cup and then leveled off with a knife.

▼ Measuring Liquids ▼

If you're measuring liquids, you can see what you're doing better if you use a Pyrex or clear plastic measuring cup with a spout. Set the cup on the counter and pour liquid in until it reaches the appropriate marked line. Bend over and look through the side of the cup to check that your measurement is accurate. Spouted cups (available in 1-cup, 2-cup and 4-cup sizes) have extra room at the top so you won't spill the measured liquid on its way to the bowl.

▼ Mixing Batter ▲

Don't overmix the batter once you've added the flour because the dough will become tough. The only time you want tough dough is when you're making bread.

▼ Positioning the Oven Rack ▲

When you're baking pies, cakes or cookies, position the oven rack in the middle groove so that the heat will circulate evenly.

▼ Don't Trust—Verify ▲

Whenever you're baking a new recipe, check the oven periodically. Don't just assume that the cooking time is correct. Even moms make mistakes.

▼ Measuring Butter ▲

Sticks of butter and margarine have tablespoon measurements printed on the wrapper. So instead of cramming them into a measuring cup and then scraping them out again, simply slice off the number of tablespoons needed:

1 cup butter/margarine = 2 sticks = 16 tablespoons
½ cup butter/margarine = 1 stick   = 8 tablespoons
¼ cup butter/margarine = ½ stick   = 4 tablespoons

Chocolate Strawberries / Oranges

SERVES: 2

Preparation Time: 15 minutes (*strawberries*) or 20 minutes (*oranges*)

Waiting Time: 30 minutes ▼ Rating: Easy

IT'S BECOME A TRADITION to spend Christmas afternoon peeling oranges and dipping them in chocolate to make that night's dessert. Not much cooking skill is involved in peeling oranges, and there's even less in washing strawberries. Nevertheless, my mom had me doing this because she didn't want to get orange peel under her fingernails. After a couple of Christmases, I started teaching my young cousin how to do this so I didn't have to get the peel under *my* nails.

The idea of dipping strawberries in chocolate came about one night when my girlfriend and I were eating a box of chocolates and came upon a strawberry filling. We decided to experiment with covering real strawberries with chocolate. We later tried apple slices, and they didn't taste as good. Bananas were okay. Experiment with your favorite fruit. My girlfriend likes pickles. Maybe I'll surprise her one day with a chocolate version. But why waste good chocolate?

1 basket strawberries (about 12 strawberries)

or

2 navel oranges (see Mom Tip 1)

1 cup (6-ounce package) semisweet chocolate chips

If using strawberries, wash them and slice off and discard the top ¼ inch of each strawberry—a quick way of removing the stems. Pat them dry with paper towels. If using oranges, peel them and separate them into sections. Remove any white fibers but leave intact the membrane enclosing the orange flesh. Set aside (see Mom Warning).

If you're dipping oranges, place a large piece of wax paper on a baking sheet or flat tray and set aside (**see Mom Tip 2**). The dipped strawberries can be set directly on a serving plate.

In your smallest pot, begin melting the chocolate chips over low heat, stirring continuously. The moment they have melted, remove the pot from the heat. For the strawberries, by hand, quickly dip the pointed end of each berry into the chocolate, holding on to the cut end with your fingers, immersing about two-thirds of the fruit. Stand each coated strawberry on its cut surface. It will look like a miniature chocolate-capped mountain.

For the oranges, quickly dip the segments into the chocolate, immersing two-thirds of the fruit. Place the dipped pieces on the wax paper to harden.

If the remaining chocolate in the pot begins to harden, warm it over low heat. Don't let it boil, or it will become granular and bitter. Chocolate burns easily. If it seems too thick or won't coat the fruit smoothly, add 1 teaspoon butter or margarine and stir until melted. Mix well and continue dipping the fruit.

Refrigerate the chocolate-coated fruit for 30 minutes, or until the chocolate has completely hardened. Then cover the fruit with foil or plastic wrap so that it doesn't dry out, and refrigerate until just before serving.

Mom Tip 1
▼

Navel oranges, which are available from November through June, can be easily divided into sections, making them very suitable for dipping. They are seedless. You can recognize them by their bellybutton-like marking. Juice oranges, on the other hand, have many seeds and are hard to separate.

Mom Tip 2
▼

Wax paper is very useful; otherwise, the chocolate oranges may stick to the plate.

Mom Warning
▼

Chocolate does not stick well to wet surfaces, so it's important that the fruit be completely dry before it's dipped. Pat it dry with a paper towel, if necessary.

Chocolate Chip Wedges

SERVES: 1-4

Preparation Time: 10 minutes ▼ Cooking Time: 30 minutes ▲ Rating: Very Easy

THIS GIGANTIC CHOCOLATE CHIP COOKIE will serve 3 or 4 people for about 10 minutes or 1 person for about ½ hour.

¼	cup (½ stick) butter or margarine
½	cup sugar
½	cup light or dark brown sugar
1	large egg
½	teaspoon vanilla extract
1	cup flour
1	teaspoon baking powder
½	teaspoon salt
1	cup (6-ounce package) semisweet chocolate chips

Place one of the oven racks in the middle position, and preheat the oven to 350 degrees.

To save time on cleanup, I cook and bake in the same container. Place a metal—not glass—pie pan on a stove burner over low heat. Melt the butter or margarine right in the pan. As soon as it's melted, turn off the heat.

Add the two sugars and stir thoroughly. Add the egg, vanilla, flour, baking powder and salt and stir until they are well combined. Mix in the chocolate chips, making sure they are well distributed through the batter (**see Mom Warning**).

Bake for 30 minutes, or until the top of the "cookie" browns and begins to pull away from the sides of the pan. Cool on a rack. Serve cut into thin wedges. Or you can cut it into any shapes you want: squares, figure-8s . . . .

Mom Warning

▼

The batter doesn't taste very good.
Even Kevin says so.
But the wedges do.

Fudge Pie

SERVES: 8-10

Preparation Time: 15 minutes ▼ **Cooking Time:** 20 minutes

Waiting Time: At least 3 hours ▲ **Rating:** Very Easy

FUDGE PIE, FUDGE PIE, FUDGE PIE. Repeat this like a mantra in times of personal crisis. Eating Fudge Pie can be quite therapeutic as well.

The first time I made Fudge Pie, I burned it. That was my mom's fault because she mistyped the baking temperature. I ate it anyway, and it was pretty good despite its ultracrunchiness. When I made it again, I checked the oven every five minutes to make sure I wasn't going to burn it again. Fudge Pie deserves my closest attention.

11	tablespoons (1 stick + 3 tablespoons) butter or margarine + more for greasing pan
3	squares unsweetened chocolate (see Mom Warning)
1½	cups sugar
⅓	cup flour
2	large eggs
2	teaspoons vanilla extract
¼	teaspoon salt
1	cup chopped walnuts

Place one of the oven racks in the middle position and preheat the oven to 350 degrees.

Melt the butter or margarine and the chocolate in a small pot over very low heat, stirring constantly. Remove the pot from the heat and set aside.

Combine the sugar and flour in a large bowl. Add the eggs and mix well. Add the vanilla, salt and walnuts and mix again. Add the melted chocolate mixture and mix until thoroughly combined.

Heavily rub the bottom and sides of an 8- or 9-inch pie pan with butter or margarine. Pour the chocolate mixture into the pie pan. Bake for 25 to 35 minutes, or until the pie is dark but not burned at the edges. Insert a knife into the center of the pie after 25 minutes; if it comes out clean, it's done. If not, cook another 2 minutes and test again. Continue this procedure until the pie is done.

Remove the pie from the oven and cool on a rack. Cover with plastic wrap or foil and refrigerate for several hours or overnight. It does not taste good warm. Serve it cold, cut into thin slices.

Mom Warning

▼

Don't confuse unsweetened chocolate with semisweet.
Both types of chocolate come in flat boxes with each ounce
of chocolate individually wrapped. Make sure you use unsweetened
chocolate in this recipe or you will definitely have a disaster.
Unsweetened chocolate is bitter to the taste. Semisweet chocolate,
which is what chocolate chips are made of, requires much less sugar
than unsweetened chocolate. I once made the mistake of using
semisweet chocolate instead of unsweetened in a fudge recipe.
The end result was so sickly sweet that I had to
throw it out. It was a very sad occasion.

Chocolate Chip Cookies

MAKES: 36 COOKIES (*depending on how much batter you eat*)

Preparation Time: 10 minutes

Cooking Time: 18 minutes (*6 minutes per baking sheet*) ▼ **Rating:** Easy

IT'S 4 A.M. AND THE DESIRE HITS ME. As others sleep, I tiptoe to the kitchen, careful not to make a sound and thereby betray my weakness when in the clutches of a cookie. I gather the ingredients together in a bag, stick the food processor under my arm and creep stealthily out to the remotest part of the house. Putting the food processor under a blanket to muffle the sound, I make the batter. I don't bother to bake. I just eat out of the bowl. My name is Kevin M. and I am a chocolate chip cookie dough addict.

1	cup (2 sticks) butter or margarine, softened to room temperature, + more for greasing baking sheets
1	cup dark brown sugar
½	cup sugar
1	large egg
1	teaspoon vanilla extract
2¼	cups flour
1	teaspoon baking powder
1	teaspoon baking soda
¼	teaspoon salt
2	cups (12-ounce package) semisweet chocolate chips (see Mom Tip)

Place one of the oven racks in the middle position and preheat the oven to 350 degrees.

Mix the butter or margarine with the two sugars in a mixing bowl or food processor until well blended.

Add the egg and vanilla and mix again. Add the flour, baking powder, baking soda and salt and mix until well blended. Add the chocolate chips and mix thoroughly. I do this last procedure by hand with a spoon—the sooner I can start tasting, the better (**see Mom Warning**).

Lightly rub 1 or 2 baking sheets with butter or margarine, or use nonstick sheets. Drop 12 small spoonfuls of cookie mixture on each sheet, 3 cookies per row in 4 rows. Bake each baking sheet, one at a time, for 6 minutes. The cookies will be brown but not dark brown. They will look not quite done, but by the time they look done on the top, they're burned on the bottom. They will firm up as they cool.

After you remove the baked cookies from the oven, let them cool on the sheet for 3 minutes, then transfer them with a spatula to a cooling rack. Let the baking sheet cool for 1 minute before reusing so the batter doesn't melt. Store the cookies in a tightly covered cookie jar.

Mom Tip 1

▼

You could add 1 cup walnuts
when you add the chips, but we don't
because they get in the way.

Mom Warning

▼

With the current concern about
the possibility of getting salmonella
poisoning from eating raw eggs,
if you plan to eat the raw batter you
might consider using egg substitute
(available in the frozen food
or refrigerated section of the
grocery store) instead
of an egg.

Chocolate Chip Cake

SERVES: 10-20 (20 NIBBLERS, 10 PIGS)

Preparation Time: 20 minutes ▼ Cooking Time: 40-45 minutes ▲ Rating: Easy

ANY DESSERT that can fill a 9-x-13-inch pan has to be worth consideration. But this cake has more going for it than just volume. It can be eaten at any hour of the day because it's a coffee cake. Don't let the chocolate chips fool you. This cake is perfect with bacon and eggs!

Cake

½	cup (1 stick) butter or margarine, softened to room temperature, + more for greasing pan
1	cup sugar
1	cup sour cream (regular or light)
2	large eggs
1	teaspoon vanilla extract
2	cups flour + 1 teaspoon for dusting pan
2	tablespoons unsweetened cocoa powder
1	teaspoon baking powder
1	teaspoon baking soda
½	cup semisweet chocolate chips

Topping

¼	cup (½ stick) butter or margarine
½	cup flour
½	cup dark brown sugar

1   tablespoon unsweetened cocoa powder
½   cup semisweet chocolate chips

Cake: Place one of the racks in the middle position and preheat the oven to 350 degrees.

If using an electric mixer or mixing by hand, put the butter or margarine and sugar in a large bowl and mix with the mixer or beat with a wooden spoon until smooth and creamy. Add the sour cream, eggs and vanilla and mix just until blended. Add the 2 cups flour, cocoa, baking powder and baking soda and mix just until blended. Mix in the chocolate chips. If you mix the batter too much, the cake will be tough.

If you own a food processor, put the butter or margarine and sugar in the food processor bowl. Briefly process until well blended. Add the sour cream, eggs and vanilla and pulse about 20 seconds, or until the mixture is well blended. Add the 2 cups flour, cocoa, baking powder and baking soda and pulse just until blended. Add the chocolate chips and blend 5 seconds.

Lightly rub the bottom and sides of a 9-x-13-inch baking pan with butter or margarine. Add the remaining 1 teaspoon flour and swirl it around, coating the buttered surfaces. This coating keeps the cake from sticking to the pan. Pour the batter into the cake pan.

Topping: Cut the butter or margarine into pea-size bits in a medium-size bowl. Add the flour, brown sugar and cocoa; toss gently. Spoon evenly over the top of the cake. Sprinkle on the chocolate chips.

Bake for 40 to 45 minutes, or until the cake pulls away from the sides of the pan and a cake tester or knife comes out clean when inserted into the center (**see Mom Warning**). Remove the pan from the oven and cool on a rack. Serve cut into squares.

Mom Warning

▼

Check the cake to see if it's done
when you start to smell it because some
ovens cook faster than others.

Grandma's Brownies

MAKES: 15-16 BROWNIES, EACH 2 INCHES

Preparation Time: 15 minutes ▼ Cooking Time: 30-35 minutes ▲ Rating: Easy

THERE IS SOMETHING MYSTERIOUS about brownies. A hundred people could follow the same recipe and each person's batch will come out different. My first attempt came out too dry because I didn't have the right pan. I got creative, divided the batter into two bread pans and overbaked both. But even if they didn't taste as good as Grandma's, how bad could they be? They were still chocolate.

½	cup (1 stick) butter or margarine + more for greasing pan
3	squares unsweetened chocolate (see Mom Warning for Fudge Pie, page 247)
2	large (or 3 small) eggs
1½	cups sugar
1	cup flour + 1 teaspoon for dusting pan
¾	teaspoon baking powder
½	teaspoon salt
1½	teaspoons vanilla extract
¾	cup chopped walnuts

Place one of the oven racks in the middle position and preheat the oven to 350 degrees.

Melt the butter or margarine and chocolate in a small pot over very low heat. Remove from the heat and set aside to cool.

Beat the eggs thoroughly in a large bowl. Use an electric mixer if you have one. Otherwise, a fork will do. Add the sugar gradually and mix thoroughly. Add the cooled chocolate mixture and mix again. Add the flour, baking powder and salt and mix well. Add the vanilla and walnuts and mix again.

Lightly rub the bottom and sides of a 10-x-6-inch or 8-x-8-inch pan with butter or margarine. Add the remaining 1 teaspoon flour and swirl it around, coating the buttered surfaces. This keeps the brownies from sticking to the pan (see Mom Tip). Pour the batter into the pan.

Bake for 30 to 35 minutes, or until a cake tester or knife comes out clean when inserted into the center. Remove from the oven and cool on a rack. Cut into squares and serve. Store in a closed container or wrapped in foil.

Mom Tip
▼

To prevent the baked brownies from sticking
to the pan, you can also try the wax paper trick.
After you've greased and floured the pan, cut a piece
of wax paper to fit the bottom of the pan.
Place it in the pan and wipe it with a bit of oil or margarine.
Pour in the batter. After the brownies have baked and then cooled
for about 10 minutes, loosen the edges with a knife and
invert the pan onto a plate. The brownies will emerge
in one large piece. Pull off the wax paper and
cut the brownies into squares.

Chocolate and Vanilla Pound Cake

SERVES: 10–12

Preparation Time: 30 minutes ▼ Cooking Time: 1 hour ▲ Rating: Not So Easy

Desserts used to be the only recipes I would cook. My repertoire included toast, cereal, frozen pizza, Chocolate Chip Cookies, Chocolate Chip Cake and this pound cake, which I even went out and bought a special pan for. Even though I can now cook main dishes, I'm sure to bake Chocolate and Vanilla Pound Cake as often as I can. You can't abandon your roots.

¾	cup semisweet chocolate chips
1	cup (2 sticks) butter, softened to room temperature, + more for greasing pan
1	cup sugar
4	large eggs
2	teaspoons vanilla extract
1¾	cups flour + 1 teaspoon for dusting pan

Place one of the oven racks in the middle position, and preheat the oven to 350 degrees.

Melt the chocolate in a small pot over very low heat, stirring constantly. Do not let it boil or it will become granular and bitter. Chocolate burns easily, so be careful. Remove the pot from the heat and set aside.

If using an electric mixer or mixing by hand, put the butter and sugar in a large bowl and mix with the mixer or beat with a wooden spoon until smooth and creamy. Add the eggs and vanilla and beat just until incorporated. Add the 1¾ cups flour and mix just until blended. If you mix the batter too much, the cake will be tough.

If you own a food processor, put the butter and sugar in the food processor bowl. Process until smooth.

Add the eggs and vanilla and process until well blended. Add the 1¾ cups flour and pulse just until blended, about 10 seconds. If you process a very long time, the cake will be tough.

Transfer half of the batter to a separate bowl and set aside. Add the melted chocolate to the remaining batter and mix or pulse just until blended.

The ideal cake pan to use is a springform pan—a deep, round pan, 8 or 9 inches in diameter, with a bottom that can be separated from the sides (if you don't have one, **see Mom Tip 1**). Lightly rub the bottom and sides of the pan with butter (**see Mom Tip 2**). Add the remaining 1 teaspoon flour and swirl it around, coating the buttered surfaces. This keeps the cake from sticking.

Spoon half of the chocolate batter into the bottom of the pan. Add half of the plain batter, then the remaining chocolate batter, then the remaining plain batter. Shake the pan several times to spread the batter around.

Bake for 50 to 60 minutes, or until a cake tester or knife inserted halfway into the center of the cake comes out clean (**see Mom Warning**). Remove the cake from the oven and cool on a rack.

When the pan is cool enough to touch, run a knife around the sides of the cake, loosening it from the pan. Remove the sides of the pan; this is the unique quality of a springform pan. Remove the pan base by sliding a knife under the cake, or just serve the cake with the base in place. This cake keeps well in the refrigerator but tastes better at room temperature. Serve it cut into thin slices.

Mom Tip 1

▼

If you don't have a
springform pan, use a loaf pan,
which typically measures
9-x-5-x-2¾ inches.
A 1- or 2-quart casserole
dish will also work.
To get the cake out of the pan,
**see Mom Tip for Grandma's
Brownies, page 253.**

The baking time may vary slightly,
so begin testing after 45 minutes.
If you mistakenly overbake the
cake and it tastes too dry, serve it
with ice cream on top.

Mom Tip 2

▼

Use the paper from the sticks
of butter to grease the pan.

Mom Warning

▼

Some ovens cook faster
than others, so you might
want to check to see if the
cake is done after 45
minutes, just in case.
Some ovens cook slowly,
so the cake may need to bake
for an extra 10 to
15 minutes.

English Walnut Pie

SERVES: 6-8

Preparation Time: 15 minutes ▼ Cooking Time: 45-50 minutes ▲ Rating: Easy

IT'S RARE THAT I'M SATISFIED with a dessert that has no chocolate in it. My friends consider me a chocolate lunatic. Thus, this recipe goes against everything I believe. But I do find this pie really tasty. And despite the lengthy list of ingredients, it's extremely simple to make, especially if you don't have to roll out your own pie crust.

My mom confessed she'd had many disasters making her own crusts before she discovered Pillsbury Pie Crusts. If she takes this shortcut, why shouldn't I? I'm a firm believer in hassle avoidance. In any case, who eats pies for the pie crust? It's just there to keep the filling from falling on the floor. However, this crust actually happens to taste good.

1	Pillsbury Pie Crust
3	large eggs
1	cup light corn syrup
1	teaspoon vanilla extract
½	cup sugar
½	teaspoon ground cinnamon
¼	teaspoon ground nutmeg
¼	teaspoon salt
2	tablespoons butter
1	cup walnut pieces (see Mom Tips 1 and 2)
1	tablespoon flour

▼

Place one of the oven racks in the middle position and preheat the oven to 400 degrees.

Following the directions on the pie crust box, line a 9-inch pie pan with the crust, smoothing it into place, and set aside. Do not bake.

Mix the eggs, corn syrup, vanilla, sugar, cinnamon, nutmeg and salt in a large bowl. Cut the butter into small pieces and add. Mix well with a fork. The filling will look lumpy.

Chop the walnuts into ¼-inch pieces. Add the flour to the walnuts and mix thoroughly so that the nuts are covered with flour. Add the mixture to the bowl. The flour coating prevents the nuts from lumping together. Stir the mixture thoroughly and pour into the pie crust.

Bake for 15 minutes. Turn down the oven temperature to 350 degrees and bake for another 30 to 35 minutes, or until the pie begins to brown. A layer of nuts will have risen to the top. Remove from the oven and cool on a rack. Serve the pie when it has reached room temperature. It is also good cold (**see Mom Tip 3**).

Mom Tip 1
▼

Walnut pieces are much
cheaper than walnut halves.
Store any leftover walnuts in a tightly
closed container in the freezer,
and they will keep
indefinitely.

Mom Tip 2
▼

You can make this pie
with pecans, which cost more
but have a similar taste.

Mom Tip 3
▼

English Walnut Pie
keeps well in the refrigerator
for several days.

BLUEBERRY PIE

SERVES: 6-8

Preparation Time: 10 minutes ▼ Cooking Time: 35-40 minutes ▲ Rating: Not So Easy

THE FIRST TIME I MADE THIS, it turned out more like blueberry soup than blueberry pie. The filling was very runny and unattached to the crust. The reason: I failed to use tapioca. I didn't have any, and my mom suggested I substitute cornstarch instead. I guess I should have used more. Tapioca absorbs liquid like a sponge.

2	Pillsbury Pie Crusts
4	cups fresh blueberries or two 12-ounce boxes frozen blueberries (not thawed)
1	cup sugar
¼	cup quick-cooking tapioca (see Mom Tip 1)
½	teaspoon ground cinnamon
¼	teaspoon ground cloves
¼	teaspoon salt
2	tablespoons lemon juice
2	tablespoons butter or margarine

Place one of the oven racks in the middle position and preheat the oven to 425 degrees.

These crusts come two to a box and are located in the refrigerated section of the grocery store, next to the tubes of refrigerated biscuits. Follow the directions on the package for "filled pie crust," placing 1 crust in a 9-inch pie pan and smoothing it into place. Set aside with the other still-wrapped crust.

To make the filling, pour the blueberries into a large bowl and sort through them, removing and discarding any still-attached stems. Add the sugar, tapioca, cinnamon, cloves, salt and lemon juice and mix well.

Transfer the contents of the bowl to the pie pan and gently shake the pan so the berries spread out evenly. Cut the butter or margarine into 8 pieces and arrange on top of the berries.

Place the second pie crust on top of the berries and fold the edge of the top crust under the edge of the bottom crust. Pinch the crusts together the whole way around the pan. Press a fork around the crust edges, about ½ inch into the pie. This should seal the crusts and keep blueberry juice from leaking out. With a knife, make 4 or 5 slashes in the top crust to allow steam to escape.

Bake for 10 minutes. Turn the oven temperature down to 350 degrees and bake for another 25 to 30 minutes, or until the crust has nicely browned. Remove from the oven and cool on a rack (**see Mom Warning and Mom Tip 2**). Serve warm or at room temperature.

Mom Tip 1

▼

Tapioca is usually located
next to the Jell-O.

Mom Tip 2

▼

Cooling the pie on a rack
instead of on a flat surface allows
air to circulate underneath it.
This prevents the crust from
becoming soggy.

Mom Tip 3

▼

If the blueberry filling
is too runny, serve the pie in a
bowl, top it with vanilla ice cream
and pretend that was your
intention all along.

Mom Warning

▼

I still have a scar on my hand from where hot,
sugary blueberry juice leaked on me when I took
this pie out of the oven. So be careful.

Foods to Keep on  Hand So You Won't Starve

Must-Have Staples

Bread

Butter

Cheese

Chicken broth (canned)

Eggs

Flour

Garlic

Ketchup

Margarine

Mayonnaise

Milk

Mustard

Oil, corn

Oil, olive

Onions

Potatoes

Rice

Salad dressing

Salt

Soy sauce

Spaghetti

Sugar

Tomatoes (canned)

Tuna

Vinegar

Useful-But-Not-Desperate Staples

Aluminum foil

Baking powder

Baking soda

Brown sugar (dark)

Chocolate chips

Cornstarch

Hot pepper sauce

Parmesan cheese

Plastic wrap

Pickles

Relish

Salsa

Scallions

Tortillas (keep frozen)

Vanilla extract

Worcestershire sauce

Must-Have Spices

Dried basil

Black pepper

Dried oregano

Red pepper flakes

Useful Spices

Bay leaves

Cayenne pepper

Celery seeds

Chili powder

Curry powder

Dried dill

Dried parsley

Dried thyme

Garlic powder

Ground cinnamon

Ground coriander

Ground cumin

Ground ginger

Dry mustard

Paprika

KITCHENWARE

You can survive with one all-purpose pot, as the pioneers did, but cooking is much easier if you have a selection that includes these:

Pots and Pans

▼ Small (1-quart) pot: rice, vegetables, reheating small amounts of food

▼ Medium (3-quart) pot: soups

▼ Big (6-8-quart) pot: pasta, corn on the cob

▼ Small (8-inch) frying pan: eggs, fried sandwiches

▼ Big (10- or 12-inch) frying pan: fried or stir-fried dishes

▼ Wok: stir-frying

▼ Roasting pan with rack: roasted meats

▼ Small (1-quart) oven-proof dish—dips, reheating leftovers in the oven

▼ Baking sheet

▼ Pie pan

▼ Pot lids

Handy Kitchenware

Can opener

Colander—for draining pasta so noodles don't slither down the drain

Cutting board

Garlic press

Grater

Kitchen scissors

Knives—paring (3-inch), serrated (9-inch), chef's (8-inch)

Measuring cups (plastic or metal) in ¼ cup, ⅓ cup, ½ cup and 1 cup sizes

Measuring spoons

Meat thermometer

Mixing bowls

Plastic storage containers

Pot holder

Potato peeler

Pyrex measuring cup

Rotary eggbeater

Rubber spatula

Slotted spoon

Soup ladle

Spatula

Timer

Tongs

Wire cooling rack

Wooden spoon

MENUS FOR ENTERTAINING

There are many considerations to putting a menu together:
▾ The dishes are complementary in taste. ▾ They aren't all the same color.
▾ They don't require all day to prepare. ▾ The cooking techniques are varied: Don't fry everything.
▾ They don't require conflicting oven temperatures. ▾ Seasonal foods aren't served out of season.
▾ There's no tricky last-minute preparation.

▾	▾
Shrimp Cocktail (*page 36*)	Gazpacho (*page 50*)
Roast Beef and Yorkshire Pudding (*page 186*)	Fresh Baked Salmon with
Greek Roast Potatoes (*page 134*)	Garlic Mayonnaise (*page 232*)
Al Dente Asparagus (*page 148*)	Spinach Spheres (*page 162*)
English Walnut Pie (*page 256*)	Chocolate and Vanilla Pound Cake (*page 254*)

▼

Mediterranean Vegetable Soup (*page 58*)
Greek Roast Leg of Lamb (*page 189*)
Greek Roast Potatoes (*page 134*)
Athenian Green Beans (*page 156*)
Chocolate Strawberries (*page 242*)

▼

Baked Ham (*page 199*)
Potato Salad (*page 78*)
Corn on the Cob (*page 152*)
Better-Than-the-Deli Four-Bean Salad (*page 68*)
Chocolate Chip Wedges (*page 244*)

▼

Mexican Seven-Layer Dip (*page 32*)
Roast Turkey with Stuffing (*page 224*) and Gravy (*page 228*)
Real Mashed Potatoes (*page 135*)
Basic Broccoli (*page 150*)
Chocolate Oranges (*page 242*)

▼

Sauerbraten (*page 184*)
Parsley Rice (*page 142*)
Roasted Vegetable Platter (*page 164*)
Fudge Pie (*page 246*)

▼

Antipasto (*page 22*)
Garlic Bread (*page 26*)
Spaghetti Bolognese (*page 101*)
Tossed Salad
Chocolate Chip Cookies (*page 248*)

▼

Spicy Bean Dip (*page 30*)
Chicken Fajitas (*page 208*)
Fresh Fruit Salad (*page 80*)
Chocolate Chip Cookies (*page 248*)

▼

Waldorf Salad (*page 77*)
Plum-Basted Pork Roast (*page 191*)
Parsley Rice (*page 142*)
Al Dente Asparagus (*page 148*)
Blueberry Pie (*page 258*)

▼

Chinese Hot and Sour Soup (*page 44*)
Teriyaki Chicken (*page 222*)
Plain Rice (*page 141*)
Vegetable Stir-Fry (*page 166*)
Grandma's Brownies (*page 252*)

Vegetarian Dinners

▼

Cheese Easies (*page 24*)
Vegetarian Chili (*page 169*)
Tossed Salad
Chocolate Chip Cake (*page 250*)

▼

Nachos (*page 34*)
Vegetable Omelet (*page 118*)
Baked Stuffed Potatoes (*page 132*)
Chocolate Strawberries (*page 242*)

▼

Egg and Onion Soup (*page 46*)
Crunchy Black Bean Salad (*page 66*)
Garlic Bread (*page 26*)
Grandma's Brownies (*page 252*)

▼

Fresh Fruit Salad (*page 80*)
Cauliflower with Cheese (*page 160*)
Baked Sweet Potato (*page 130*)
Chocolate Chip Cookies (*page 248*)

▼

Grilled Mushrooms (*page 158*)
Spaghetti with Pesto Sauce (*page 104*)
Garlic Bread (*page 26*)
Blueberry Pie (*page 258*)

Vegetarian Dishes

Appetizers

Antipasto (*page 22; omit the salami and tuna*)
Cheese Easies (*page 24*)
Garlic Bread (*page 26*)
Guacamole (*page 28*)
Spicy Bean Dip (*page 30;
use vegetarian refried beans*)
Mexican Seven-Layer Dip (*page 32*)
Nachos (*page 34*)

Soups

Cheddar Potato Soup (*page 42*)
Chinese Hot and Sour Soup (*page 44*)
Egg and Onion Soup (*page 46*)
French Onion Soup (*page 48*)
Gazpacho (*page 50*)
Hearty Lentil Soup (*page 52*)
Mexican Corn Chowder (*page 54*)
Mediterranean Vegetable Soup (*page 58*)

Salads

Sandwiches/Quesadillas/Pizzas

Pastas

Eggs/Cheese

Potatoes/Rice

Vegetables: Side and Main Dishes

Tofu

INDEX

About the Authors

Kevin Mills, a recent graduate of Cornell University, just survived his first year in an apartment containing a room he eventually discovered to be the kitchen.

A lifelong eating expert whose first word was "more," Kevin had his earliest hands-on association with the food industry the summer he spent bagging groceries at a nearby supermarket. He acquired further professionalism the following summer as a register clerk at a taco takeaway. Among his published works is a series of newspaper reviews critiquing local hamburger joints.

Nancy Mills is a home economics graduate from Cornell University, a journalist and the person responsible for feeding Kevin during his first 18 years. A newspaper and magazine writer whose work has appeared in the *Los Angeles Times*, *Cosmopolitan*, *Saturday Evening Post*, *Ladies Home Journal*, and *USA Weekend*, Nancy also co-owns a newspaper feature syndicate. She has published three books: **Home Economists in Action** (Scholastic), **Beverly Hills 90210—Exposed** (HarperCollins) and **Melrose Place—Off the Record** (HarperCollins).